Stop "Living with Grief"

Stop "Living with Grief"

BE SET FREE 100%

Jim Gardner

2015

Table of Contents

Preface

When I wrote *Trading Pain for Peace* in 2008, my goal was to provide a simple overview of the prayer-based counseling method that I had learned, so that others could use it. As I began working at a mental health clinic and continued applying the basic principles of "Emotional Healing Prayer" to my clients, I began encountering a broader range of mental health issues including substance abuse, depression, posttraumatic stress, anxiety disorders, and marital problems. The more experience that I gained the more excited I became about "Emotional Healing Prayer" and the more I wanted to share what I had learned with others.

As I began using a prayer-based approach with my clients I was astounded to see how many of them had underlying issues of grief and anger. I began searching the research literature to learn how effective secular approaches were in helping those with grief and was amazed to learn that the top experts in the field of grief counseling admitted that nothing seemed to help resolve "normal grief." It was then that I began to realize that a book had to be written to share how the Lord is able to take away our grief. As I searched the internet for other books on the subject I found many books that tell people how to live with their grief but none that taught how to overcome it completely.

The more experience that I gained in helping grieving people, the more I came to realize that grief is often connected to feelings of sadness, anger, and shame, and that grieving people need to know how to deal with each of these emotions in order to find complete freedom from the emotional impact of their losses. Soon I came to realize that these same four emotions are at the root of depression, addictions, traumas, marital problems and almost all mental disorders. This book addresses each of these four emotions and how to overcome them through prayer. It is focused primarily upon how to help people overcome their losses, but it is also very effective in helping people overcome other mental health disorders.

Grief has a profound impact on many people, both Christians and non-Christians, and my intention with this book is to provide a book that can be used in a group study to enable individuals to identify and resolve the underlying emotions connected to their losses. For this reason I have included study questions at the end of each chapter to enable group study leaders to lead a discussion with class members about their own losses. Not all of the study questions should be discussed with the class each week but the class leader should select the questions that he/she believes will be most useful for enabling the class to openly discuss their feelings. It is recommended that the class participants be provided a copy of the book before the first class and be instructed to read one chapter prior to each class so that they will be able to discuss it. There are also some application suggestions at the end of each chapter to help guide the group members in praying through their grief-related issues systematically as they go through the class, so that they will find freedom and peace. Just reading this book will not take away the pain, because mere insight is insufficient to resolve the emotional pain. However, those who commit themselves to applying the concepts discussed and praying about their grief will find tremendous relief.

A series of 12 video sessions are being developed to go along with each chapter in the book and can be purchased at tradingpain.com. It is recommended that the video for each chapter be shown to the group at the beginning of each weekly session. In these videos I introduce the key concepts of each chapter and discuss technical issues that may be difficult for group leaders to teach. Each video is approximately 20 minutes long and supplements the content of each chapter in the book. It is recommended that at least 90 minutes be allocated for each class session so that there will be adequate time for sharing and discussion and allow time for prayer with someone in the group, if there is a volunteer. If the group leader is willing to pray with class members it will maximize the impact that the group sessions will have upon the class members.

My hope and prayer is that this book will enable many readers to find freedom from their losses, and then they will get excited about Jesus and about prayer and spread this to others. If enough people do this perhaps we will see the same phenomenon that occurred in the early New Testament church where "Everyone kept feeling a sense of awe" (Acts 2:43) and where the believers were so excited about the Lord that they "turned the world upside down" (Acts 17:6, KJV).

Jim Gardner, Ph.D.
tradingpain.com

Acknowledgements

I am deeply grateful to Dr. Ed Smith of Theophostic Prayer Ministry for the biblical and clinical foundations he laid for me through his seminars, conferences, videos, and writings. In 2002 I attended an 8-hour video seminar on Theophostic Ministry and was profoundly impacted by the teachings of Dr. Ed Smith. I was very excited to learn the basic prayer principles of this ministry and a few months later I attended an Advanced Theophostic Ministry seminar in Campbellsville, Kentucky where I learned how to apply the basic principles to helping people with severe emotional disorders.

Since I was a licensed professional counselor I availed myself of every opportunity to attend conferences and training seminars offered by Dr. Smith and I did everything I could to become competent and skilled at Theophostic Prayer Ministry. What I presented in *Trading Pain for Peace* and am presenting in this book is not Theophostic Prayer Ministry, but it is built upon the foundational prayer principles articulated by Dr. Ed Smith.

When I first learned about Theophostic Ministry I tried to spread it by giving copies of Dr. Smith's book *Healing Life's Deepest Hurts* to pastors, and inviting them to attend a Theophostic Ministry Basic Training video conference. I soon became discouraged to see how few people continued using these principles after attending a conference. Many people seemed to be overwhelmed by trying to learn them, and sometimes I found it very difficult myself to apply the basic principles of the ministry to some of my clients. I tried to simplify the principles for myself and found myself praying more with clients about their anger and grief than their belief-based feelings, which I found more difficult to address. This simplification process developed into what I now call "Emotional Healing Prayer." Although Emotional Healing Prayer was built upon the concepts I learned from Theophostic Prayer Ministry, it is not Theophostic Prayer Ministry because it deviates in a number of ways from it.

I am also very deeply indebted to my wife, who has assisted me, edited, proofread, and offered many helpful suggestions to me in the development of this book. Without her support and persistent efforts this book would not have been written. She has been my strongest supporter and ally over the years since I first learned these prayer principles and began to teach them to others. I am very grateful for having such a competent helpmate and loving wife.

There are many other friends and ministry partners who have encouraged me substantially in my writings and seminars and who have become very competent in using this prayer ministry with others. I am grateful to Melissa Weis who graciously volunteered to proofread the manuscript for this book to facilitate the message of the book. There are many ministry friends in Oklahoma, Kansas, Arkansas, and Tennessee who have encouraged me by their support, and the numbers of these supporters and ministry partners is growing daily. Some of them warrant special acknowledgment due to their steadfast support including Josh Holmes from Kansas, Nicole Mann from Tennessee, Judy Day from Arkansas, and Nathan Tuck from Oklahoma. Each of these individuals has encouraged me repeatedly by their excitement about the ministry and by their stories about their personal victories and the victories of others with whom they have prayed.

Of course, I am most grateful to our Heavenly Father and the Lord Jesus Christ who is our "Wonderful Counselor, Mighty God, Eternal Father, Prince of Peace" (Isaiah 9:6). The more that I see Him setting people free from their grief, anger, shame, and emotional bondage, the more excited I am about Him, and the more I love Him and want to lead others to Him. I pray that this book will help many people to find peace and joy in Him and to worship Him.

CHAPTER 1

Hope for the Hurting

As I began writing this book a man came to me for counseling. I had never met him before, and as I invited him into my office he was cordial but was obviously distraught. As I settled into my chair I asked him what brought him to the clinic. With a serious expression he looked me directly in the eyes and said, "I just lost my seventeen-year-old boy."

I was shocked at his blunt statement and replied, "I'm sorry to hear that. When did this happen?" He told me that it had just been six weeks earlier. I expressed my condolences again and tried to empathize by saying, "Losing a child is one of the most painful things anyone can experience. How have you and your family been handling it?"

He told me that he had gone back to work a week and a half after it happened, but his wife had still not returned to work, and his daughter had dropped out of college for a semester to come home for the funeral and to help her parents. I asked him what had happened to his son, and he told me that his son was healthy and had no known medical problems. One morning his son's alarm clock went off, but he did not come out of his room, so the father went to wake him up. When he entered his bedroom his son was sitting in a love seat with his head slumped over, so he went over to him and touched him to wake him up, and he was cold. The man was shocked and raised his son's eyelids and saw that his eyes were rolled up into his head and he knew that he was dead.

This father wept as he told me about this tragic account. He pulled out his I-phone and showed me a video of his son playing the guitar. I was impressed with his talent, and with what a mature young man he appeared to be. I commented about what a nice young man he was and how difficult this must be for the father. He said that his son was well-liked and that so many people came to his funeral that several hundred people had to stand outside the church for the service.

This man was unashamedly sorrowful and wept as he spoke of his son. I was impressed with his ability to talk about his son and to weep without embarrassment. With the heavy grief and sadness this man was carrying I felt burdened to offer some relief to him in this first session rather than wait until our next session, which was my more typical procedure. Eleven years earlier I would have had nothing to offer him, but during the last eleven years I had seen hundreds, and maybe even thousands, of people find genuine healing after a significant loss. I decided to take a risk and share with this father what I had learned about grief.

"If you would have come to me twelve years ago, I wouldn't have had anything to offer to you but some empathy, because I tried for twenty-five years to help people with grief and nothing worked," I told him. "But about eleven years ago I learned a way to help people overcome their grief, and in the last ten years I've seen hundreds of people find healing from their grief and sadness from losses. I would be glad to share it with you if you are interested," I offered cautiously. He looked at me with an expression of sincere interest and hopefulness and said that he was receptive to anything that might help him.

I shared with him the first time I ever saw someone experience healing from grief, so he would understand how he could find relief from his grief, then I quickly added, "I know this sounds too simple to be true, but I promise you that it works and I have seen hundreds of people released from their deep sadness through this process. However, I realize that this is a little different because it is a faith-based process, and if you are uncomfortable with it I will not mention it again." He stated that he went to church as a child and he believed in God and he was willing to try anything that might help him.

We spent the next thirty minutes talking about his son and what he missed about him. He wept and he laughed as he recalled each fond memory of his son and identified thirty-one things he missed about him. I led him in a prayer and he poured out his heart to the Lord. When we were finished I prayed and asked the Lord if there was anything that He wanted this man to know. "He's okay; and he's with God," the father told me. I asked him how he felt as he thought about his son, and with a smile he told me that he felt peaceful and a lot lighter. He told me that when he had entered my office he was angry and depressed because his son had been taken from him, but now he felt no anger or grief, but just felt peaceful and calm. I saw him a week later and he was still doing well but needed to release a little more sadness, but after that his grief was gone and he required no more help.

This story is not an isolated case of emotional healing of grief. I have seen hundreds and hundreds of people set free from grief over the last twelve years and I see this type of healing on almost a daily basis. However, I spent twenty-five years unsuccessfully trying to help people resolve their painful losses prior to learning how to do this. This book is not designed to help you learn to live with grief, but to help you learn how to be completely set free from your grief, so that you can give glory to God for His goodness, and so you can help others to be set free also.

The Pain of Grief

Grief is one of the most painful emotions that humans experience, and it often has a profound impact upon them. I experienced a personal example of this when my mother-in-law came to live with my wife and me a few years before she passed away. She was not able to converse much, so I wasn't really close to her, but I respected her for being a godly woman who did a good job raising her three children alone. Her health declined steadily due to diabetes and a series of minor strokes and she was eventually placed on hospice care in our home. One evening as we turned her in her bed I saw her eyes roll up into the top of her head and I felt a sudden dread of imminent death. I was certain that she was going to die that evening.

Before we went to bed I checked on her and she was weak but alive. I tearfully prayed for her and asked her forgiveness for not spending more time with her or being more caring, and then I went to bed. I woke up early the next morning before anyone else and I jumped out of bed and went to check on my mother-in-law. When I saw her I could tell that she had died, and my heart was suddenly overwhelmed with a deep sadness and sorrow that caused me to burst into tears and to weep heavily. I went to wake up my brother-in-law who was staying with us in expectation of his mother's pending death, and I called out his name, but I was so emotional that I could barely talk. I choked out the words that his mother had died. I was amazed at the gut-wrenching strength of my sorrow for the loss of a woman I barely knew, but this was the first time I had ever witnessed a death or had a death occur in my home.

I always had the impression that grief was only painful for those who were weak in faith, and that godly people could deal with it with seren-ity. I have met a few people who experienced a traumatic loss in their life as children who were able to release it to the Lord and to experience serenity, by the grace of God. But, in the Bible, grief is portrayed as a very painful experience, even for the most godly people. Abraham grieved deeply for the loss of his wife Sarah who died at one hundred twenty-seven years of age, and in Genesis 23:2 we are told that "Abraham went in to mourn for Sarah and to weep for her." Genesis 23 is devoted to the account of how Abraham bought a piece of land for Sarah's burial, and chapter 24 is devoted to the story of how Abraham found a wife for his son Isaac to comfort him after his mother's death (24:67). Abraham was a man of great faith and is held up as an example of a man of faith in Hebrews 11:8-12, but he grieved deeply for the loss of his wife Sarah in her old age. Grief is very painful, but it is very normal, and it is not unspiritual or immature to feel deep pain and sadness at the death of a loved one.

When Jacob died, the "Egyptians wept for him seventy days" (Genesis 50:3) and the household of Joseph and his brothers and his father's household traveled to a burial site purchased in the land of Canaan, beyond the Jordan river, and "they lamented there with a very great and sorrowful lamentation; and he observed seven days mourning for his father" (Genesis 50:10). This was a very lengthy, extensive funeral process that demonstrates the strength of sorrow and grief that Joseph felt for the loss of his father. Although he was a very godly man, his grief was very intense.

Many other Biblical accounts corroborate the normality of grief and the intensity of pain that often accompanies the loss of a loved one. In Exodus 12 the Lord smote the first-born sons of the Egyptians as the last of ten plagues. Exodus 12:30 says, "Pharaoh arose in the night, he and all his servants and all the Egyptians; and there was a great cry in Egypt, for there was no home where there was not someone dead." This was the final plague that led Pharaoh to release the Israelites, which he had stubbornly refused to do until then. The death of his first-born son broke his stubborn heart to motivate him to submit to God's command to let His people go.

David was a man after God's own heart (Acts 13:22) but he made some terrible mistakes in his life which led to some painful losses. He had a son named Absalom who rebelled against him and tried to take over his kingdom by force. The faithful men who supported David fought against the armies of Israel that Absalom commanded, and 20,000 men died in that battle (2 Samuel 18:7) in a great slaughter, and Absalom was killed by Joab, the commander of David's army. When David was informed about the defeat of his enemies his only concern was for his son Absalom, and when he heard that Absalom had been killed he wept bitterly. 2 Samuel 18:33 tells us, "the king was deeply moved and went up to the chamber over the gate and wept. And thus he said as he walked, 'O my son Absalom, my son, my son Absalom! Would I had died instead of you, O Absalom, my son, my son!'" David was so grief-stricken over the loss of his son that Joab eventually went to speak with him and explain that thousands had fought for him and given their lives, and that he needed to address them as king and express his gratitude for their sacrifice so that they would not all turn against him. David's grief overwhelmed his awareness of his responsibility as king.

In his recent book entitled *Nearing Home*, Billy Graham wrote about his experience with the loss of his wife, Ruth, four years ago. In a section called "living with grief" he wrote, "As I write this it has been four years since Ruth went home to be with the Lord. I feel her loss more keenly now...I have asked myself why this is the case; after all, shouldn't our grieving over the loss of a loved one fade as time passes? Yes, it should...and in some ways it has for me. But in other ways it hasn't, nor do I expect it to." (Graham 2011) His struggle with grief illustrates that grief is normal and can be very painful, and it also demonstrates that mature Christians struggle with grief as much as young Christians and unbelievers. There is no question that grief is presented in the Bible as a very normal experience that can be extremely painful. The experience of deep pain does not diminish the spiritual maturity of the person or indicate that they lack faith.

Normal Grief and Complicated Grief

The pain connected to grief can be intense, but it is regarded as normal by mental health professionals until it persists for more than twelve months. When daily struggles with grief last more than six months, it is considered to be abnormal and has been called Complicated Grief, Traumatic Grief, or Prolonged Grief. The *Diagnostic and Statistical Manual of Mental Disorders, Fifth Edition* (DSM-5) which was released in 2013 added, "Persistent Complex Bereavement Disorder" to the official list of the American Psychiatric Association's (APA) diagnoses. The diagnostic criteria for this disorder includes "persistent yearning/longing for the deceased... intense sorrow and emotional pain in response to the death... preoccupation with the deceased..." or "preoccupation with the circumstances of the death" that persist at least 12 months after the death in the case of bereaved adults plus the inclusion of several additional criteria (p. 789-790).

Grief researchers suggest that only about 15% of all grief cases become complicated; the other 85% of grief cases are gradually resolved over time. This means that most losses do not result in long-lasting symptoms or symptoms that have a profound impact upon the individual. However, there are many long-lasting effects that are not generally recognized by individuals, such as feelings of anger, depression, or substance abuse problems that are a direct result of traumatic losses, so the estimate of 15% is probably an underestimation of the complicated grief cases. The impact of grief is far greater than implied by this conservative figure, when all of the emotional and mental health consequences are considered.

The Impact of Grief

In 2002 I attended a workshop that was put on by a pastoral counselor, and I learned that it was possible for people to be completely healed of their grief. When I first learned how to help people overcome grief, I was counseling teenage boys at a group home for boys. My job was to do a social history on these boys to identify the underlying reasons for their behavioral problems, and then to provide them counseling for their problems. I was amazed to discover that approximately 60% to 70% of these young men with "conduct disorders" or "oppositional defiant disorders" or "substance abuse disorders" had some significant losses that led to their behavior problems.

One young man that I counseled was a very quiet, pleasant boy who had never been in trouble until the preceding year. When I met with him I learned that his problems began after his older brother had died from an asthma attack in the previous year, while sleeping in the same room with him. His brother's death was traumatizing to him because he was very close to his brother and idolized him, so he lost his best friend when his brother died. Later that same year, this young man's mother died also. With these two losses this young man became very depressed, began using drugs, and quit going to school, so he was sent to this boys' home for help.

He was always very pleasant and quiet and respectful toward the staff, but then he participated with some other boys who broke into the medicine cabinet and stole some pills to take. I offered to help him but he stubbornly refused to talk with me about his grief and he continued to use drugs and pills which got him into trouble. Since he was not making progress in this group home, he was eventually transferred to another boys' home nearby, but I also worked part-time at this other group home, so he was shocked when he saw me at this new facility. He behaved the same way in this new facility; he was pleasant and respectful but whenever he received a pass to go home to visit his father he got caught drinking or using drugs. His father bought him a brand new, red Ford Mustang that he drove to the boys' home to show his friends, but the following weekend when he went on a home visit, he and his cousin got drunk and wrecked this car and totaled it.

This young man returned the following week to the facility and was wearing a neck brace due to his injuries. He was fortunate that he or his cousin was not killed in the car wreck. When I saw him for counseling I asked him if he was ready to talk about his grief yet. He said that he was ready, so we talked and prayed and he was able to release his grief over the loss of his brother and mother. His grief was suddenly lifted and he was able to stay out of trouble and complete the program.

After I had been working in group homes for several years, my wife and I moved to Oklahoma and I began working for a mental health clinic. I was amazed to learn how many people with mental health issues had experienced significant losses prior to the onset of their mental disorders. For about six months I conducted intake interviews on every new client that came for help, and I found that over half of them reported that their losses were a significant contributing factor in the onset of their mental health problems.

Then I began working in an inpatient substance abuse program and interviewed everyone who entered the treatment program. I found that 68% of all the clients who were admitted into this program reported having a significant loss prior to their initial abuse of drugs or alcohol. As part of the intake interview I also inquired about their history of physical abuse, emotional abuse, sexual abuse, parental neglect, witnessing violence, out-of-home placement, adoption, and traumatic losses. I found that the second most frequent form of childhood trauma experienced by the substance abusers in this program was emotional abuse, which 52% of them reported, and the third most frequent form of childhood trauma experienced by these clients was witnessing violence, which 41% of them reported. Thirty-six percent of them also reported having been physically abused and twenty-three percent of them reported having been sexually abused prior to the onset of their abuse of alcohol or drugs. So by far, the most significant trauma these men had experienced prior to the onset of their substance abuse was the traumatic loss of someone close to them.

Next, I began working at a behavioral health clinic and seeing a case-load of clients with a broad range of mental disorders. I was amazed to discover that over half of them reported having experienced a significant loss prior to their development of any form of mental illness. I began searching the professional literature to get some statistics on this issue. Kenneth Kendler, M.D., and Carol Prescott, Ph.D., conducted a study that is sometimes referred to as the "Virginia Twin Study" of over 9,000 twins in Virginia to assess the role of genetic and environmental factors in mental disorder. This study documented their findings including the fact that 87.4% of all depressed individuals interviewed as part of this study indicated that their depression began after they experienced some form of loss (Kendler, Myers and Zisook 2008). That was a shocking finding that corroborated my personal clinical experience that depression was usually rooted in some form of loss.

In 2010 an article was published in the December issue of *Psychology Today* entitled, "The Road to Understand Depression Goes Through Bereavement." Psychologist Jonathan Rottenberg, Ph.D., came to the same conclusion as I had, that depression is usually rooted in unresolved feelings of grief and that we cannot help people overcome their depression without helping them deal with their losses.

Grief not only leads to substance abuse, conduct disorders, and depression, but it often leads to anger problems, violence, and marital problems. It has a tremendous impact on people's lives because it is so painful and there is no known way for mental health professionals to relieve people of their grief and losses.

Types of Losses

When talking about grief, most people think of the loss of a loved one through death. But there are other types of losses that are painful as well and can have the same impact, or even a greater impact than a death. In addition to loss by death, losses can also include the loss of a relationship, the loss of a job, the loss of property, the loss of health, or the loss of one's dreams. All of these types of losses feel bad and can result in deep emotional pain.

One of the most common types of grief experienced by individuals in our society is the loss of one's family through divorce. Divorce impacts not only the divorcing couple, but the children as well. Those who have experienced a divorce understand that it can be extremely painful and lead to depression and suicidal ideas. Children whose parents divorce are often devastated by the loss of their family unit, the loss of one of their parents, and the loss of financial and social stability. The good news is that all of these types of losses can be resolved in the same way, using the same technique, so whatever your loss is, you can benefit from this book and course.

Hope for the Brokenhearted

There is a pervasive sense of hopelessness in our society when it comes to dealing with the issue of grief. One of the most widely-held beliefs about grief is that "you will never get over it, but it will just weaken over time." In my thirty-five years in the mental health profession I have heard many discussions about grief, and this statement is made frequently. I spoke with a professor of a counseling school and tried to share with him that I had found a way for people to resolve their feelings of grief, and he immediately responded with the comment, "The question is: does one ever truly get over grief?" His question was really a statement to counter my claim that I had found something that works.

The Virginia Twin Study, cited earlier, found that 87% of all depression is rooted in some type of loss, so the sense of hopelessness about grief is also found in the attitude toward depression. If mental health professionals cannot help people with grief, and if depression is rooted in grief, then professionals will be unable to help those with depression. The medical community has carried this hopelessness a step further and has promoted the concept that depression is a brain disorder or a chemical imbalance and so the only solution is medication. The pharmaceutical companies were the first ones to introduce this concept and are happy to promote this belief and to invest in the production of more and more medications to help numb our feelings, as they make billions of dollars on medication sales. This belief is not only endorsed by secular physicians, but by Christian physicians as well, since they are trained in the same schools, and it has spread almost universally to pastors of conservative churches as a result.

On April 5, 2013 Rick Warren, Pastor of Saddleback Church in California and author of *The Purpose-Driven Life*, tragically lost his son who committed suicide. For nearly four months he withdrew from public life until he returned to the pulpit on July 28, 2013. Among his remarks at that time, he said, "I was in shock for at least a month. I prayed for 27 years for my son's healing; it was my number one prayer..." He stated that his son had the best counselors and doctors available to him, and his experience had sparked in him a desire to minister to people struggling with mental illness. He offered the following encouragement to his listeners: "If you struggle with a broken brain, you should be no more ashamed than someone with a broken arm. It's not a sin to take meds. It's not a sin to get help. You don't need to be ashamed" (Warren 2013).

Although it is true that we should be honest about our struggles and it is not a sin to get help or take medications, his statement supports the sense of hopelessness that pervades our society and the belief that Christianity has nothing more to offer than the world does. I attended a meeting where another pastor publicly shared his experience with depression and admitted that he had been repeatedly hospitalized for suicidal depression and had received ECT shock therapy treatments, and stated that he still takes six pills every day and has suicidal thoughts every day. He stated that he does this because he has a "brain disorder" and he will have to do this the rest of his life. While I admire his honesty and courage, such statements from spiritual leaders lead people to feel hopeless about their emotional struggles.

The Scriptures flatly contradict such comments when they teach us, for example, that "the fruit of the Spirit is love, joy, peace..." (Galatians 5:22). This statement from the apostle Paul makes it clear that the Holy Spirit is able to take away our depression and sorrow and anger, because it is impossible to have peace and also to be full of anger, sadness, grief, or depression. Peace is incompatible with anger, grief, and sadness. One who is full of anger or grief or sadness is not experiencing the peace of God. In 2 Thessalonians 3:16, Paul makes an even stronger statement when he says, "Now may the Lord of Peace Himself, continually grant you peace in every circumstance."

The Lord Jesus said in John 14:1, "Let not your heart be troubled; believe in God, believe also in Me." The word "troubled" means to be stirred up or agitated. An agitator in a washing machine is that device in the middle of the machine that stirs the water so that the clothes can be cleaned. Jesus is telling us not to be agitated but to believe in Him, so that we will experience His peace. He repeated this statement in John 14:27 where He said, "Peace I leave with you; My peace I give to you; not as the world gives, do I give to you. Let not your heart be troubled, nor let it be fearful." He is teaching us here that we can experience His peace in the midst of difficult circumstances, and it is His will that we learn how to live in such peace.

The apostle Paul was constantly persecuted and mistreated in his ministry. He was stoned, imprisoned, shipwrecked, beaten, and destitute at times. In 2 Corinthians 4:8-9 he wrote, "we are afflicted in every way, but not crushed; perplexed, but not despairing; persecuted, but not forsaken; struck down, but not destroyed." He goes on to say in verse 16, "we do not lose heart, but though our outer man is decaying, yet our inner man is being renewed day by day." In 2 Corinthians 7:6 he wrote, "God, who comforts the depressed, comforted us by the coming of Titus." During his missionary journey in Acts 16, Paul and Silas were thrown into jail illegally and had their hands and feet placed in the stocks, and the scriptures in verse 25 say that, "about midnight Paul and Silas were praying and singing hymns of praise to God, and the prisoners were listening to them." Paul did not give in to despair in the most difficult circumstances. He even wrote in Romans 15:13, "Now may the God of hope fill you with all joy and peace in believing, that you may abound in hope by the power of the Holy Spirit."

Paul was a remarkable man and he set a high standard for believers to follow. It is difficult to follow in his footsteps, but it is encouraging to see that he was not the only one who was able to maintain peace in the midst of difficulties. In Acts 13:50-52 we see that after the Jews instigated persecution against Paul and Barnabas and drove them out of their district, the other believers were also encouraged. Verse 52 says, "the disciples were continually filled with joy and with the Holy Spirit."

All of the disciples in Pisidian Antioch were experiencing joy and peace in spite of the persecution that they were enduring.

A mature Christian man who was a leader in his church pointed out to me that some hymn writers struggled with depression, and he asked if the Lord allowed them to experience such depression so that they could write great hymns of encouragement. My answer was that it is not God's will that we ever feel hopeless, because He is the God of hope, and when we feel hopeless we are not experiencing the fruit of the Spirit in our lives. Most people do experience hopelessness at times, and many mature Christians experience depression also, but we cannot give in to the belief that there is no solution to depression other than taking pills because we have a chemical imbalance.

Most of us will struggle at times, but we must never give in to the world's belief that there is no hope, because we have a God of hope who is always with us, to strengthen us, and to give us His peace in all circumstances. The Lord "is able to do exceeding abundantly beyond all that we ask or think, according to the power that works within us" according to Ephesians 3:20, and that applies to healing us of our negative emotions. Grief can be very painful, and it is normal to experience deep pain and sadness when we lose a loved one, but the Lord does not want us to be stuck there for long. He is able to take our grief from us and carry it for us, and we will examine how He can do that in the next chapter.

Discussion Questions

1. What led you to attend this class and how do you hope you will benefit from it?

2. What is the most difficult loss that you have experienced in your lifetime?

3. How did that loss affect you immediately after it happened, and how does it still affect you today? How often do you think about that loss, and how do you feel emotionally when you think about it?

4. If it was possible to get rid of your painful feelings of grief while retaining all of your memories of your loved one, would you want to do that?

5. How many of you have heard it said that you never get over grief; it just weakens over time? How does that make you feel when you think about your own losses?

Personal Application

In order to benefit from this class or from this book, you must apply the principles being presented in it to your personal life. Just reading this book or hearing stories about others being set free will not help you find freedom. For this reason, most chapters will end with a personal application assignment that should be completed before you go further in the book or course. Even if you primarily want to learn how to help others, it is very critical that you begin with finding some freedom in your own personal life before trying to help others. Once you experience some freedom you will be able to use this to teach others how to find freedom from grief.

Your first assignment is to make a list of every significant loss that you have had in your life. Some people have many losses and others have very few so it varies widely from person to person. At this point you are not encouraged to think about these losses, just to recognize the losses that you have had which might be affecting you in some way. In the next chapter you will learn how you can release them, but you must first be completely honest in doing this assignment.

My Significant Losses

1. _____

2. _____

3. _____

4. _____

5. _____

6. _____

7. _____

8. _____

9. _____

CHAPTER 2

How to Overcome Grief

In 2002 I attended a workshop that was presented by a pastoral counselor and I heard some remarkable stories of how people could be set free from feelings of fear, helplessness, hopelessness, anger, grief, and shame simply through the use of prayer. This workshop was truly revolutionary for me professionally and personally. I had four degrees and had worked in the mental health field for twenty-five years and I had never heard of any way to help people overcome grief. I certainly had never seen anyone healed completely of any deep grief. As I began to apply what I had learned, I saw the Lord miraculously and quickly set people free from many types of emotional struggles, and I became more and more excited. Then a Christian couple asked me to see their 12-year-old son to help him deal with the death of his cousin.

I agreed to meet with the boy and I reviewed my notes from the workshop to remember the steps needed to help set people free from their grief. However, my notes were confusing and unclear so I reviewed the video conference session where the presenter spoke about how he was able to be set free from his grief over the loss of a child. He devoted only about fifteen minutes of the 8-hour seminar to discussing "Truth-based Emotions" which included anger, grief, sadness, and disappointment, and I viewed these fifteen minutes several times and tried to remember the steps that he presented for releasing grief. He told a personal story of how he and his wife lost their first child who died suddenly, as an infant, from an undetectable brain tumor, and how the pain from this loss persisted more than ten years afterwards. By praying about this loss this man and his wife were gloriously and immediately set free from their grief and sadness.

I tried to remember the steps that he described having taken but I could not remember them all and I felt very anxious and inadequate to help the twelve-year-old boy. I listened to him, asked questions to understand more fully his feelings, and encouraged him to try to pray about it and take the steps recommended by the pastoral counselor in the video. I'm sure that I was not very helpful, however, because I could not even understand the steps identified in the video. So, I went carefully through the video repeatedly and tried to simplify the steps. The best that I could understand, there appeared to be two simple principles that the pastoral counselor was using to help people overcome their grief. First, he encouraged them to be completely honest about the things they missed about the person who died, and secondly, he prayed with them and asked the Lord to take their grief from them and carry it for them.

My First Grief Healing Session

My wife and I moved to Nashville, Tennessee, and I opened a private counseling practice to begin to practice using this exciting new prayer-based approach to counseling. To supplement my private practice I began counseling some young men in a Christian group home for boys, where young men were placed who were disruptive in their homes or getting into legal problems. A young man arrived at this facility who was homeless and not attending school, and we were informed that he had just lost his best friend three weeks earlier. His best friend, it turned out, was his cousin. They had lived together and were like brothers, doing everything together.

When this young man arrived at the group home, I met with him and asked him how he was handling the loss of his cousin, and he told me that he was not handling it very well. He said that he thought about him all the time, and it hurt so badly that he felt a knot in the middle of his chest, and he motioned to his chest. I asked him if he would like to get rid of that pain, if it was possible to do so. He said, "Yes. I'd do anything to get rid of that pain."

I explained to this young man that there were two things he needed to do in order to get rid of his emotional pain. First, he needed to be completely honest about his grief and identify everything that he missed about his cousin. So, I asked him what he missed about him and he said, "I miss hanging out with him and talking with him, I miss his goofy sense of humor and all the goofy things he said and did." He told me that he missed hunting with him and fishing with him, and he continued identifying everything that he missed about his cousin until I had a long list of items.

Secondly, I asked him if he would be willing to say a simple prayer and tell God everything he missed about his cousin, then ask Him to take his grief and carry it for him. He said, "Sure, I can do that. I'm not a religious person but I believe in God and prayer." So, I led him in a prayer and went through the list of things he missed about his cousin, and then he prayed, "Lord, I miss all these things about my cousin, but I am tired of feeling this sadness and grief. So right now I choose to give them to You, and I ask you to please take them from me and carry them for me. In Jesus' name I pray, Amen."

After the prayer I told him to think about his cousin and tell me how he felt. He thought about his cousin and said, "When I said that prayer I felt like a load was lifted from me. I feel okay." I said to him, "That's good. Now think about all of these things you have been missing about him and try to stir up those sad feelings again." He reflected again on his cousin and said, "I just feel peaceful and calm." I told him that was good, and I released him to return to his room saying, "Let's see how you do now."

The following morning I saw this young man mowing grass, so I approached him and he turned off the lawn mower. I asked him how he was doing. He said, "You know what? I slept all night long without any problem. That was the first time in three weeks that I have been able to sleep!" "That's great!" I replied. "While you have been mowing this morning have you been thinking about your cousin?"

"Yes I have," he said with a smile. "But I've only been remembering all the good times we had together." He told me that the knot he had in his chest was no longer there and he felt peaceful and calm. I was very pleased but a little unsure how long this would last, since I had never seen this happen before, so I had weekly counseling sessions with this young man for the next five months while he was still at this group home. He never had any more periods of sadness or depression about the loss of his cousin after that.

His grief was completely healed in a 30-minute prayer session. The result was an immediate termination of his feelings of grief, his inability to stir up the pain afterwards while thinking about his loss, the removal of the physical pain in the chest, the ability to sleep without thinking about his cousin, and the long-term freedom from negative emotions when thinking about his cousin.

Steps to Overcoming Grief

STEP ONE: *Be completely honest about your loss.*

The first step in overcoming grief is to be completely honest about your loss by making a list of everything you miss about the person or loss that makes you feel bad. It is very important that you be completely honest and thorough when you pray about your grief, because if you are not willing to be honest about your pain the Lord will not force you to do so; you simply will be unable to release your feelings.

STEP TWO: *Ask the Lord to take your grief from you.*

The second step is to say a simple prayer, telling the Lord everything you miss about the person or loss, and then sincerely ask Him to take the sadness from you and carry it for you. When people pray through their grief they need to allow themselves to experience their grief, which usually means they show some emotion. This is an important part of the process of being honest with the Lord, because when we suppress our emotions and try to control them we do not give them fully to the Lord. Even though the person may have already ventilated about their feelings when making the list, they must give them to the Lord and sincerely ask Him to take them. When they do this, the Lord supernaturally takes their grief from them.

In order to assess the grief of the young man mentioned previously I asked him to try to stir up his negative feelings. When working with individuals to set them free from grief, my goal is to help them experience 100% peace and calm when they think about their friend or loved one. When someone has been completely healed of their grief, they are able to think about the deceased person and talk about them without getting stirred up and tearful. They will continue to think about the deceased person and miss them, but there will not be a painful sadness or grief that overwhelms them or makes them feel like crying. The best way to assess this is to ask the person to think about their loved one and see how they respond.

When there is Still Unresolved Grief

About 90% of the time when I pray with someone about their grief over a loss, they report complete relief after one prayer. Sometimes, however, when I ask the person how they feel when they think about their loved one, they report that they still feel some grief and miss the person. This usually means that I missed something the first time around and I need to identify what I missed, make another list, and pray again. When this happens, I simply ask, "What still makes you sad when you think about them?" They may repeat something they had previously identified, or they may begin mentioning something new about the person that they miss.

Clients who miss important components of their grief, do so for several reasons. First, it happens when a client prays quickly through a list of items but two or three of the items are so painful that they need more time to elaborate upon them and focus on them. As they talk more about those items that still bother them, more aspects of the loss will usually surface along with some more emotions. Second, clients may overlook some significant memories when they knew the deceased person for a very long time and there are so many significant memories that they cannot remember everything at once. This happens most often when a couple has been married for a very long time. In such cases, the surviving spouse may need to pray several times to resolve all of their grief. Third, it happens sometimes when a client prays on his own and only comes up with a small number, such as three to seven items, for his list. Most people seem to end up with twenty or more specific items on their list of things they miss about the deceased person, and many people need some help in learning how to be completely honest and thorough in listing the things they miss about their loved one.

Thinking and talking about someone they have lost will tend to stir up a client's feelings and make them feel bad, so there is a strong tendency for people to avoid doing this without some encouragement. I often explain to clients that it is very important to be completely honest and thorough when making their list, because when they are suppressing their emotions and refusing to experience them, God will not force His way into their mind to take their painful memories from them. However, when they are completely honest about their feelings and lay them out before the Lord and ask Him to take them and carry them, then He is willing and eager to take them and carry them. This is why the Lord said, "Come to Me, all who are weary and heavy-laden, and I will give you rest" (Matthew 11:28).

Helpful Questions

To help clients to be thorough about what they miss about their loved one when they want to pray on their own, I suggest that they answer the following questions:

- What activities do you miss doing with the person?
- What do you miss about his/her personality?
- Did he/she have a good sense of humor that you miss?
- What do you miss about their physical characteristics?
- What are some of your favorite memories of the person?

As the individual answers these questions, they may tell stories about the person that make them laugh or cry. This is part of the process of being honest, so it is important for them to do this, but since I usually see people for one-hour sessions I have a time limitation and I cannot allow them to tell stories endlessly. I summarize what they miss about the person and then ask, "Okay, is there anything else that you miss about them?" I continue with this process of eliciting memories and feelings until they come to a point of closure on the list. Then I ask them, "Would you be willing to say a simple prayer and tell the Lord these things that you miss about your friend, then ask Him to take your grief from you?" If they say they would, I ask permission to lead them in a prayer and have them repeat after me. If they are resistant to praying with me, I offer to lead them in prayer and have them silently pray after me, or to have them take the list with them and pray on their own.

Sometimes, individuals will release all of their grief, but they have other feelings that need to be resolved also. The most common emotions connected to grief and loss are sadness, anger, and shame and guilt. These emotions will be discussed separately in the chapters to follow, and each of them needs to be resolved so that the person will experience complete peace and calm after their prayer session.

"I Have Already Tried Praying"

Since that first case when I witnessed the healing of this young man's grief I have seen hundreds of other people healed just as quickly, using these same two simple steps. It works with people who have simple, normal grief and with those who have complicated grief. It works with those who lost someone a long time ago, and with those who lost someone recently. I never push it on individuals who have had recent losses; I simply tell them that I have found a way for people to release their grief and when they are ready I would be glad to share it with them.

I had an older woman come to me one time for counseling. She was a very dignified, Christian woman who was embarrassed about coming for counseling because she had never been to a counselor before, but she told me that she could not go on living like she was living. Six months earlier she had lost her oldest son, with whom she was very close. He was a grown man in his forties and he was the pastor of her church. When he died, she was devastated at his loss and saddened by the fact that he died so young.

I shared with her that I had learned how to help people release their grief through prayer, and her initial reaction was that she had already tried praying. She had prayed with her husband and with several pastors but no matter what she did her intense pain and sorrow would not leave. I explained that it was not generic prayer that I recommended but praying specifically about the things she missed about her son, and then giving her pain to the Lord and asking him to carry it for her. She said that she was willing to try it because she was so desperate to find relief.

We made a list of everything she missed about her son, and then I led her in a prayer, telling the Lord what she missed about him and asking the Lord to take her grief and pain from her. When we finished praying, I asked her how she felt. She said that she felt better about her son, but she still felt sadness about his wife and children who were struggling without him. We prayed again and gave her sadness to the Lord, and then I asked her again how she felt. She smiled and said that she felt peaceful. She was able to think about her son and not feel the heavy burden of grief that she had felt when she entered my office.

We talked about God's goodness and His desire to carry our burdens for us. As she left the room she turned and smiled and said, "He can do anything!" From that day on she did well and was relieved of the heavy burden of grief that she had been carrying for six months.

"It's Too Simple"

I have had the opportunity to share this truth with many Christians and with many pastors. I spoke with a group of about thirty pastors one time and they all seemed very receptive. Many of them thanked me sincerely for my time and for sharing this message of hope with them. I left feeling excited and anticipating that some wonderful things were about to happen. I was hopeful that these pastors would begin to teach this truth to their congregations and I would see God's awesome power manifested in churches all around the area. However, about a month later I spoke with the pastor who organized the meeting and he told me that some of the pastors said it was too simple. I only saw two of those thirty pastors after that meeting, and only one of them invited me to do some follow-up meetings at his church.

It astounds me that so many Christians and pastors are so resistant to this message of hope, and it amazes me that any Christian would object to hearing that God can heal us emotionally in such a simple manner. I tried the hard way, for twenty-five years, and it didn't work. But the Scriptures say that the Lord likes to confound the wise with the simple: "God has chosen the foolish things of the world to shame the wise... that no man should boast before God" (1 Corinthians 1:27, 29). I love to see the Lord heal the brokenhearted through this simple approach because I know it is not coming from me and my wisdom but from the Lord, and He gets all the glory!

It reminds me of the story of Naaman, the leper, who was the captain of the Aramean army. He had a servant girl who told him about the prophet Elisha, and she told Naaman that Elisha could heal him of his leprosy. So, Naaman gathered a large contingency of men and traveled to Elisha's home in Israel. When he arrived, he sent one of his servants to Elisha's door and Elisha never came out to meet Naaman; he simply told him through a servant to go dip himself in the Jordan River seven times. When Naaman heard these words he was furious and went away in a rage. Then his servants spoke to him and said, "My father, had the prophet told you to do some great thing, would you not have done it? How much more then, when he says to you, 'wash and be clean'?" (2 Kings 5:13). Then he went and dipped himself in the Jordan seven times and "his flesh was restored like the flesh of a little child, and he was clean."

The Lord likes to do great things in a simple way so that all men will know that He is God and our faith will not rest on the wisdom of men but on the power of God. I believe He has given us a simple way to help people to be healed of grief, so that we can demonstrate His power through simple prayer and He will be glorified.

Discussion Questions

1. Read 2 Thessalonians 3:16 and John 14:27. Do you think these Scriptures apply to the emotional pain of grief and loss? How does it make you feel to read these words?

2. In Matthew 11:28 Jesus said, "Come to Me, all who are weary and heavy-laden, and I will give you rest." Do you think the Lord wants us to experience peace and rest even after we lose someone very close to us?

3. If you could get rid of your feelings of grief and sadness over the loss of someone or something important to you, would you want to?

4. Share with the group the losses that you have experienced in your lifetime, and identify the ones that have been the most painful for you.

Personal Application

In the last chapter you wrote out a list of people or things you have lost in your lifetime. Your second assignment is to select one of the losses that you have experienced which still bothers you, and to write out a list of everything you miss about this person or loss. This loss could be the death of someone close to you, but if you have not had any significant losses or you believe that they are 100% resolved, then pick another loss. It may be the loss of a close friendship, a pastor who left your church, a friend who moved away, a divorce, the loss of custody of a child, or the loss of a child who left the nest to become independent or to get married. It may even be the loss of your health, the loss of a career through retirement, loss of a job through termination, or loss of a dream.

It is important to be thorough in writing out the list of things you miss about your loss, so do not cut corners in this process, but do not obsess about it. If you are not thorough you will only receive partial healing, but you can always go back and cover the things that you missed. Right now, simply take a piece of paper and write out a brief statement of each thing you miss, numbering them in a vertical list. Try to think of at least 20 things you miss about the person or loss. Then say a prayer and tell the Lord everything that you miss about this person, and ask Him to take your grief and carry it for you. This process may stir up some strong feelings of grief and loss, but it won't last long, and it is important to be honest about your feelings with the Lord. The following prayer can be used as a guideline if you find this helpful.

Sample Prayer

"Lord, when I think about _____ I miss him/her. I feel sad when I remember how he/she did _____ and said _____. But Lord, I'm tired of carrying this grief, so right now I choose to give it to You, and I ask You to please take it from me and carry it for me. So, I give it to You now in Jesus' name. Amen."

Now, think about the person and what you miss about them and see how you feel. Write down your feelings so that you can share them with others in your class. Most people report that they feel peaceful and calm, even when they think about the person. If so, thank the Lord. If you still have some grief, make a list of what still makes you feel bad or what you still miss a lot, and say another prayer.

If you have other feelings, such as feelings of sadness or anger, repeat this process with each of these emotions until you have perfect peace about the loss. When you finish this process you should have complete peace while thinking about the person you lost. If there are still some strong, unresolved feelings, this will be addressed in one of the subsequent chapters of this book.

CHAPTER 3

Why Grief Counseling Does Not Work

t is very instructive to notice that even the Lord Jesus, the perfect Son of God, experienced deep grief and sorrow at times. In John 11, when Jesus returned to Bethany where his friend Lazarus had died, the two sisters of Lazarus ran to meet him. Martha went to him first, and Jesus spoke some comforting words to her, and told her that her brother would be raised to life, but she did not understand what He meant. She returned to her sister, Mary, and told her that the Lord was calling for her, so Mary ran to meet Jesus and fell at his feet saying, "Lord, if You had been here, my brother would not have died" (John 11:32).

The Scriptures tell us, "When Jesus therefore saw her weeping, and the Jews who came with her *also* weeping, He was deeply moved in spirit, and was troubled, and said, 'Where have you laid him?' They said to Him, 'Lord, come and see.' Jesus wept." (John 11:33-35). This has to be one of the most profound statements in the Bible! It's an amazing thing that the Son of God was "deeply moved in spirit and... troubled" even though He knew that he was going to raise Lazarus from the dead in a few minutes. He was apparently so saddened to see the depth of Mary's grief that he empathized with her and wept with her. He experienced her pain and her grief just as Isaiah 53:3-4 tells us, "He was a man of sorrows and acquainted with grief; Surely He has borne our griefs and carried our sorrows" (KJV).

On another occasion, Jesus was informed about the beheading of his cousin, John the Baptist. In Matthew 14:13 the Scriptures say, "Now when Jesus heard [about John], He withdrew from there in a boat to a lonely place by Himself; and when the multitudes heard *of this*, they followed Him on foot from the cities." Jesus wanted to be alone after receiving news of the death of John, suggesting that He felt some sadness and had a desire to spend time alone with His Heavenly Father. Of course, this did not last long because the multitudes saw where He went and followed Him there in a short while.

The fact that Jesus experienced grief proves that grief is normal, as discussed previously. It also proves that grief is not the result of irrational thinking, because the Son of God did not have any irrational or distorted thinking. Jesus was the Son of God, so His thoughts were higher than our thoughts, according to Isaiah 55:9, "as the heavens are higher than the earth." Most counseling theories are built upon some form of cognitive therapy which believes that all negative feelings are the result of irrational or distorted thinking, so the efforts of most counselors are directed at trying to identify distorted thinking in order to relieve clients of their emotional suffering. Such an approach is doomed to failure when dealing with grief and loss, because grief is not a belief-based emotion based in irrational thinking. When we lose a loved one, the pain of loss is very rational, and is based upon the reality that we will not see our loved one again for a very long time, and that is truly sad.

Grief Counseling Outcome Research

After I wrote *Trading Pain for Peace* in 2008, I decided to examine the research on grief counseling to see what the experts were saying about traditional grief counseling. I found a 2003 "Report on Bereavement and Grief Research" that was written by twenty-three of the top researchers in the field of grief counseling. This report was commissioned by the Office of Prevention of the National Institute of Mental Health of the National Institutes of Health and provided a comprehensive assessment of the research on issues related to grief. The following is their conclusion: "For participants experiencing uncomplicated bereavement [normal grief], there was essentially no measurable positive effect on any variable and nearly one in two clients suffered as a result of treatment" (Genevro, 2003, p. 66). In other words, these experts unanimously concluded that there was no evidence that grief therapy helps people with normal grief, and that about half of the time the clients reported that they felt worse when they finished grief counseling than they had felt prior to their counseling. They also wrote, "Professional psychological intervention is generally neither justified nor effective for uncomplicated forms of grief" (Genevro 2003, p. 66).

In 2007, a man who is considered by many to be the leading expert on bereavement, Dr. Colin Parkes, stated "there is no evidence that all bereaved people will benefit from counseling and research has shown no benefits to arise from the routine referral to counseling for no other reason than that they have suffered a bereavement" (Stroebe, Schut and Stroebe 2007). To further aggravate the grief counseling profession, Psychologist Scott Lilienfeld of Emory University wrote an article entitled, "Psychological Treatments that Cause Harm," in which he classified grief counseling for normal bereavement as a "potentially harmful treatment" (PHT) (Lilienfeld 2007, Vol. 2, No. 1).

In reaction to these challenges to the field of grief counseling, which has numerous training programs for professionals who wish to specialize in grief counseling, some researchers vigorously contested these findings, especially the claim that "nearly one in two clients suffered as a result of treatment." However, in 2009 another study was published in the journal *Current Directions in Psychological Science*, reporting the results of another major meta-analysis. A meta-analysis is a research methodology that pools the results from multiple independent studies so that there is a larger pool of subjects, and this provides greater statistical power to the researcher to detect very small treatment effects. Robert Neimeyer and Joseph Currier pooled 75 outcome studies of grief therapies, spanning three decades of research and making this "the most comprehensive summary of the literature available." What they found was, "Consistent with the majority of smaller-scale reviews, our tests of overall effectiveness failed to yield an overly encouraging picture of grief therapies" and that "interventions failed to produce better outcomes than would be expected by the passage of time" (Neimeyer 2009).

Most mental health professionals are unaware of this research, but even some "experts" in the field are ignorant of it. I attended a workshop on "Trauma, PTSD and Grief" by a psychologist who was advertised as a "Board Certified Expert in Traumatic Stress" and who had reportedly trained "tens of thousands of people in her seminars" and had made numerous radio and television appearances. She appeared to be a very nice woman who was probably a Christian, and she spoke about some techniques that she recommended for use with clients who are suffering grief. Between seminar sessions I spoke with her personally and asked her if she was familiar with the report written by the twenty-three experts, and their conclusion that grief counseling is ineffective and appeared to harm people half of the time. She had never heard of this report and challenged their results with the statement, "Oh, I know that can't be true. I have known many fine, qualified grief counselors who do an excellent job of helping people overcome their grief." Based upon her simple impression, she just dismissed the research findings of the research experts in the field.

Another study in 2005 reported on a new therapy called "Complicated Grief Therapy" and boasted about its effectiveness. The technique involved 16-20 weeks of therapy including repeated discussion of painful memories of the deceased loved ones. Over twenty-five percent of the participants dropped out (13 out of 49). Fifty-one percent of the remaining 75% were rated as "much improved" or "very much improved," but this amounted to only 37% of the original group, since 25% dropped out without completing the program due to the emotional pain involved. Five of the completers refused to participate in retelling the story of the death and having an imaginary conversation with the deceased person because they considered this too difficult. In addition, forty-five percent of the participants in the study were taking psychotropic medications during the study, so it is impossible to know how much of the reported improvement of the participants was due to the therapy and how much was due to the numbing effects of their medications (Shear, et al. 2005).

Modern-day Miracles

In contrast to these findings, I have been using the simple prayer-based approach described in this book for the past twelve years, and have seen hundreds of individuals with both normal grief and with complicated grief set free from their painful grief reactions. In most cases these individuals have been able to find complete resolution of their grief in a single session, whether the loss occurred fifty years ago or a week ago. A few individuals have required several sessions in order to release all of the emotions connected to their grief. Given the poor outcome of traditional grief counseling approaches and the dramatic and quick resolution of grief using this approach, I believe that this prayer process for resolving grief is a miracle.

Knowing how ineffective grief counseling is, when I see people immediately relieved of their grief it reminds me of the woman in Mark 5:25-34. This woman had been suffering from a hemorrhage for twelve years, and she quietly came up behind Jesus and touched His garment. He was surrounded by a crowd, but when He felt some power being released from Him he turned and asked, "Who touched My garments?" This woman came forward with fear and trembling, and fell down before Him and told him the whole truth. She had had the hemorrhage for twelve years, and verse 26 says she "had endured much at the hands of many physicians, and had spent all that she had and was not helped at all, but rather had grown worse." With one touch of the garments of Jesus, however, she was completely set free from her affliction after she had spent all that she had on ineffective medical treatments.

This is exactly what happens frequently to people today, who believe that physicians with all of the advanced medical technology that we have today can do everything and know everything about medical conditions. However, there are many, many conditions that doctors do not understand and cannot help you with, in spite of their advanced knowledge and technology. I underwent triple by-pass heart surgery in 2004, which is a marvelous display of modern medical technology, and I am alive today because of this. However, I developed some severe pain in my left leg several years ago that was so extreme that I was unable to walk around the block with my wife. I went through extensive tests, MRIs, and many expensive procedures and no cause was ever found. These tests were very expensive and I could not have afforded them without my insurance, but all of them were ineffective in diagnosing my problem, which eventually resolved itself without any medical intervention. Other people have spent their life savings to try to help their loved ones survive some medical problem, only to lose them eventually.

In the field of mental health this happens on a regular basis. People experience problems such as depression, anxiety, or posttraumatic stress and go to therapists for a long time and never find any relief, so they begin taking expensive psychiatric medications. These medications sometimes help for a short while, but they never ultimately cure the problem, and they often lead to much more severe problems such as nightmares, violent impulses, and suicidal ideation. Then the patients are hospitalized in psychiatric facilities and placed on more expensive medications that lead to greater problems. Most psychiatric patients are told that they will need to remain on their medications for the rest of their lives, and they are encouraged to apply for disability since the medications prevent them from being able to function adequately in a job. They "endure much at the hands of many physicians and [spend] all that [they have] and [are] not helped at all, but rather [have] grown worse," just as this woman in the Bible with the hemorrhage had done. But the good news is that with one touch from the Lord, they can be completely healed, like this woman was.

The Woman who Hated Christmas

There are many people whom I have seen who have been grief-stricken and depressed over the loss of a loved one for as long as fifty years, and in a single session their grief is resolved and they are able to think about and talk about the loved one with total peace in their heart. For over forty years researchers have been trying to help people find relief from their grief with no success, so when I see people healed of their grief in a single session I realize that this is a genuine miracle.

One of my favorite cases was a woman who worked with me in a clinic. I didn't know this woman but when we passed in the hallways of the clinic we usually smiled and greeted each other. In early December of 2011 I passed her in the hallway and greeted her, and I asked her how her Thanksgiving went. She said, "Oh, it was very good. We had our entire family together and had a good time." Then she unexpectedly added, "But I'm not looking forward to Christmas."

"Really," I responded. "Why is that?" She said, "I don't like Christmas." Still curious, I tried again, "Is there a reason for that?"

"I lost my mother sixteen years ago on Christmas, and I don't like Christmas because it reminds me of her," she replied.

"Oh, I'm sorry to hear that," I said. "It takes a long time to get over losses at times. But you know, I have learned a way to help people get past their losses. If you're interested in learning more about this I'd be glad to share it with you sometime."

"Yeah, I'd like to do that" she answered.

The following week when I was at that clinic I saw her again and she said, "I'm ready to talk with you, whenever you have time." I invited her to my office and we sat down. I asked her to explain to me what happened to her mother.

"I grew up in Thailand and my mother and I were very close; she was my best friend. We talked all the time and I could talk with her about anything. She was very loving so it was hard to leave her when I moved to this country. I missed her a lot, and then one day my sister called me and told me that Mom was sick and I needed to come see her. So I bought a plane ticket, but before I got on the plane my sister called and told me that Mother had died. I never got to see her again, or say goodbye and get closure."

Certainly this was a sad experience, but I knew this woman could be helped. I explained that there were two things she needed to do. First, she needed to be completely honest about her loss of her mother and make a list of everything that she missed about her. So, she talked about her mother and all the good memories she had of her, and what she missed most about her, and I wrote all of this down. Then I explained that the second step she needed to take was to say a prayer and tell the Lord everything she missed about her mother, and ask Him to take her grief and sadness from her. I led her in a prayer, taking her through her list, and she repeated each item in her own native Thai language, with tears flowing down her cheeks as we prayed. When we finished the list she prayed, "Lord, I miss all these things about my mother, but I am tired of carrying these feelings; so right now I choose to give them to you, and I ask you to please take them and carry them for me. I give them to you now in Jesus' name. Amen."

When we finished this prayer I asked her to think about her mother and tell me how she felt. She said, "I feel peaceful and calm. I can't believe it! I have been carrying this for sixteen years and no one has told me how to do this." She was so excited and thankful that she asked if she could give me a hug before she left my office.

A week later, when I returned to this clinic again, I went to her office to check on her. I knocked on her door and she opened the door and was wearing a Santa hat. I asked her how she felt and she just smiled and pointed up at her hat. She said, "Guess what? I went out this week and bought a Christmas tree! I'm looking forward to Christmas!"

I didn't see her again for about a month until late January when I went to her office again to check on her. I asked her how her Christmas was, and she told me that she had had a wonderful Christmas and had no sadness or grief about her mother. She also said, "Last week my husband tried to take down our Christmas lights and I told him, "No, leave the lights up!" She was still celebrating Christmas a month after Christmas, after not celebrating it for sixteen years! That shows the power of the

Lord to bring complete healing of grief so that the person will no longer be affected by a loss.

Continuing Miracles

I continue to witness miracles like this on a regular basis. This week, while working on this chapter, I saw a woman who was very distraught and grief-stricken about her husband leaving her for another woman. They had been married for six years and had a child together, but had separated for several months in order to work out some problems they were having. Then her husband met another woman and told his wife that their relationship was over. She was so distraught that she began having anxiety attacks, and she was unable to sleep for more than two hours each night. I explained how she could get release from her grief through prayer, and she told me that her father had been a preacher when she was a child, and she was willing to try it, but she openly admitted that she was skeptical that it would work.

We made a list of twenty-nine things she missed about her husband, including his presence, his caring, his phone calls, and his talks with her when she was upset. She also missed watching certain TV shows together, going out on a date night each week, and his kisses in the morning and telling her that he loved her. As she talked about what she missed about him it brought tears to her eyes, and when we prayed through this list she cried even more. Then she told the Lord she was tired of carrying this grief and she asked Him to take it from her and carry it for her.

After her prayer I asked the Lord if there was anything He wanted her to know. "You're OK," was what came to her mind. She said she felt better but still had some sadness that her husband was moving on without her, so we prayed about this and she gave her sadness to the Lord. Again, I asked the Lord what He wanted her to know and she began smiling. She said she heard the words, "I have a plan." She said that this gave her some hope and this is what her deceased mother used to tell her all the time.

When I asked her how she felt, she said she felt no grief or sadness, but she felt lighter and she felt hope. She had been very skeptical that the prayer process would work but was amazed afterwards at how much better she felt. She said with a big smile, "I feel a lot better than I have in a long time!" She had entered the room with a heavy heart and heavy grief, but she left with a light heart and a smile on her face.

I also saw a man who lost his wife to cancer three months ago. They had been married for thirty-three years and raised three children together. He said that they never fought; she was always cheerful and encouraging to him, they enjoyed studying the Bible together and singing. At about age forty, she was diagnosed with cancer and began treatments, which extended her life for nine years, but destroyed her body and mind. She went from being a beautiful woman to a weak, shriveled woman who could not take care of her basic needs, and this man had to quit his job to take care of her in her last several months. She lost her mental abilities, also, and did not even know who he was most of the time. She died a slow, painful death three months ago and he became very depressed, cried all the time, and became so angry at times that he wanted to tear things up. He said that he could only sleep about two hours per night, and he even developed doubts about God.

I shared with this man how the Lord could set him free through prayer, and he said he was willing to try it because he said, "I'm tired of hurting." We made a list of things he missed about his wife. He missed her positive personality, her smile and laughter, her cooking, her touches, her love and affection, and her scent. He told me how he missed going for long walks with her, playing the guitar for her and singing with her, praying together, and joking with her. He missed raising their children together, and he missed seeing her beautiful hair, her eyes, and her beautiful smile. We made a list of twenty-five things he missed about his wife, and then we prayed and told the Lord these things and asked Him to take his grief from him and carry it for him.

When we were finished, I asked the Lord if there was anything that He wanted him to know. The man said, "She's with Him now and He's taking care of her. She's all right and she's waiting for me." Then I asked him what he thought about that and he said, "It's amazing! I prayed so many times over this but never felt any better! Now I feel calm."

This man was experiencing "normal grief" and had already prayed on his own but did not know how to pray for relief. With a little help, he is now experiencing God's peace again. The Lord does not want us to be stuck in our grief; He wants us to learn to be completely honest with Him and give our burdens to Him so that He can carry them for us.

Since I know what the research says about grief counseling and since I failed for twenty-five years in my efforts to help grieving people, I believe that these are genuine miracles that the Lord is performing as I pray with my clients. The grief researchers say that nothing helps those experiencing grief, but I see these types of miracles almost daily, showing that the Lord can do for us what no counselor, psychologist, doctor or medication of any kind can do. He heals our broken hearts and gives us His peace, even when we are experiencing a painful loss.

Discussion Questions

1. Do you think it is a true miracle for people to be completely healed of their grief and sadness after a single prayer session?

2. What have you experienced recently from praying about your own losses? Do you believe that a miracle occurred?

3. Is there someone here today that has already made out a list of things you miss about someone that you lost, who wants to pray right now and give your grief to the Lord?

4. As a group take a few minutes (10-15 minutes) to pray through your list of things you miss about someone and ask the Lord to take your grief and sadness from you. Ask the Lord if there is anything that He wants you to know and write down any thoughts that come to your mind. Then share with the group what you experienced and how you feel now as you think about your loved one.

5. How did it make you feel when you made your list of things you missed about a loved one and then prayed and gave your grief and sadness to the Lord?

6. After finding relief of your grief last week did you share your experience with anyone? Did your experience give you a desire to talk with others and try to help others find freedom also?

Personal Application

Think about other experiences of loss in your life and try to identify other unresolved losses you have had. Consider relationships, jobs, dreams, homes, and other losses that you have had in your lifetime and see if you have any remaining grief or sadness about these losses. If you do, then make out another list of things that you miss about that person or loss, and pray through your list, giving your feelings to the Lord. Write down your feelings and thoughts afterwards and then bring this page with you to your next class to share with the other group members.

CHAPTER 4

How to Overcome Sadness

Shortly after I wrote *Trading Pain for Peace* I was leading a Sunday School class and teaching the class how to overcome grief. Each week I would ask for a volunteer and invite class members to pray in class about some grief, and no one volunteered-- probably because they were fearful of showing any emotions to their fellow class members. However, it was a very small class and I continued to invite the class members to allow me to pray with them during class, so one woman finally volunteered. She came to class prepared, carrying a large photo album, but I had no idea what she was carrying until I asked if anyone wanted prayer and she pulled out the album and said, "Okay. Here we go; let's do it."

This woman opened up her photo album and showed us some pictures of a friend of hers who had died a few months earlier. As she showed the class pictures of her friend and her friend's family she told us that the friend had cancer and knew she was dying. This brave woman sat with her friend and held her hand as she wept and expressed fear about her salvation. She did the best she could to assure her friend of her salvation but she felt uncertain that she had done it adequately. The dying woman was terrified during her last hours of life but her friend remained at her bedside, holding her hand and crying with her until she passed away. It left her traumatized.

As she recalled this traumatic experience she wept heavily; the trauma was still very much alive within her. I explained that the first step to releasing it was to make a list of everything that she missed about her friend, so she began talking about her friend and told me what she missed about her. I wrote out a list of what she said and then asked if I could lead her in a prayer to tell the Lord what she missed about her friend. As I led her in the prayer she repeated it after me and shed tears profusely. She asked the Lord to take her grief from her and carry it for her, and then I asked her how she felt.

This woman burst into tears again and said, "I still feel bad!" I asked her what thoughts were connected to her tears and she said, "Her children are going to have to grow up without her, her husband is going to have to raise his kids by himself, she was just too young to die, and it was so sad to see how scared she was as she lay there dying!" I recognized that these were not things that she missed about her friend, but things that were sad about her friend's death. I asked her if she would like to get rid of her sadness and she said that she would, so I led her in another prayer and she gave her sadness to the Lord and asked Him to carry it for her.

After this second prayer she calmed down and quit crying. I asked her how she felt and she said that she felt a lot better. She tried to stir up her former feelings of grief and sadness but said that she felt peaceful and calm. The following week she confirmed that she still felt calm and had not felt any more sadness about her friend, and she had not lost any more sleep over her. A year later she approached me with excitement and told me that she had just gone to a one-year memorial service for her friend and she had been asked to sing a song at the service. She was able to sing without any difficulty and she said that she still felt complete calm and peace about the loss of her friend.

The Difference between Grief and Sadness

Many people would have stopped after the first prayer with this woman and concluded that it does not always work. I would have done the same if it had not been for my experience and learning that there are sometimes other emotions that are connected to grief. I asked questions to identify the reasons for her tears after the first prayer, and when she told me the thoughts that were connected to her emotions, it became clear that she had strong feelings of sadness in addition to the feelings of grief that she had.

So, what is the difference between grief and sadness? Grief, the way that I like to define it, is an intense longing for someone who has passed away or whom one has lost as a close friend. You can make a list of everything someone misses about a person, including things they miss doing with them, things they miss about their personality, things about their appearance, and things about their character. Once a person identifies all these missed items and releases them, they may still have strong feelings of sadness about the death or loss.

The following are some of the most common reasons for sadness about a death:

- The person died so young.
- They died in a slow or painful way.
- They left behind friends or family who are devastated by their loss.

- They never got to get married or have children.
- Their grandchildren will never get to meet them.
- They were unsaved and may be facing eternal separation from God.

Other reasons for sadness might include having died from a violent act, or having died shortly before or after an important event such as retirement or marriage. Help the person make a list of the reasons for their sadness, and then pray with them about these reasons and ask the Lord to take their sadness from them.

Steps for Overcoming Sadness

Sometimes people will spontaneously list things they miss about a person and things that make them sad. When this happens, you can include them together and get healing for both emotions, because they are dealt with in the same way, using the same steps.

STEP ONE: Be completely honest about your sadness.

First, have them be completely honest about the reasons for their sadness by making a list of these reasons.

STEP TWO: Ask the Lord to take your sadness from you.

Second, tell the Lord in a simple prayer the reasons for their sadness and then ask Him to take their sadness from them and carry it for them.

Ask them afterwards how they feel. If they feel no more sadness even when they try to stir it up again, then they have successfully released their sadness. But, if they report that they still feel some sadness, then ask them what still makes them sad and help them make up another list and pray again.

Fact-based Emotions

The reason that the same steps are used for sadness as are used for grief is that grief and sadness are both "fact-based" emotions that are not caused by irrational or distorted thinking. In Chapter Three we discussed "cognitive therapy," which teaches that all negative emotions are caused by irrational or distorted thinking. Many negative emotions are, indeed, caused by distorted beliefs held by the individual, such as feelings of aloneness, fear, shame, helplessness, hopelessness, and hurt. All of these emotions are belief-based emotions and are caused by distorted beliefs (or lies). Jesus never experienced these (except for true aloneness) because He was the Son of God and He could not have any irrational or distorted thoughts since He was God.

The exception was the emotion of aloneness, because He experienced true aloneness when He was being crucified and He cried out, "My God, My God, why hast Thou forsaken Me?" (Mark 15:34). Jesus was truly alone when the Heavenly Father turned His back to Him because He was bearing our sins on the cross for us. His aloneness was very painful and it was a fact-based pain, but when we feel alone it is lie-based because the Lord promises never to leave us or forsake us, (Hebrews 13:5). Even before we come to know the Lord we are told in the Scriptures that He is everywhere and that we cannot hide from Him or escape His presence (Psalm 139:7-8).

In a later chapter we will talk more about the belief-based emotions when we talk about shame. Shame is the belief-based emotion that is most often connected to feelings of grief and loss, so it is important to know how to deal with shame when trying to resolve all of your negative feelings associated with grief.

Sadness over Death of Atheist Friend

A man came to a Set Free meeting one time and shared that he had lost a friend recently who died of cancer. When he mentioned this friend, his eyes became red and it was obvious that he had some unresolved feelings of grief. So I asked him if he would like to get rid of those feelings, and he said that he would. I asked him what feelings he had when he thought about his friend. He missed his friend and felt some grief, but he was most distraught that the friend was an atheist, and so he felt some sadness because he believed that his friend was spending eternity in hell. That's truly sad to think about friends or family members being in hell, so what would you say to ease that sadness?

I made a list of the reasons for his sadness. He said that he was sad that he was not present when his friend died, his friend didn't know the Lord, he couldn't get clean himself long enough to help his friend, and his friend didn't get to see him get well and get off the drugs. We ended up with seven reasons for his sadness. Then I made a list of ten things he missed about his friend. He said he missed talking with him about everything, spending time with him, having fun together, seeing the smile on his face, hearing his laughter, and enjoying his friendship and joyfulness. I explained to this man that there were two steps to getting rid of his grief and sadness: first, he had to be honest about his feelings and write them out, and second, he needed to pray and tell the Lord what he missed about his friend, then ask Him to take it from him and carry it for him.

I asked him if I could lead him in a prayer, and he said I could. We told the Lord everything that he missed about his friend and everything that made him sad about his friend, and then we asked the Lord to take his grief and sadness and carry it for him. After we finished praying I asked him to think about his friend and tell me how he felt. He said that he felt "happiness." I asked him if he had any sadness and he said that he did feel some sadness still about his friend not knowing the Lord. So, he prayed again and said, "Lord, it makes me sad that my friend was an atheist and did not know you, and it makes me sad to think that he is spending eternity in hell. But Lord, I'm tired of carrying this sadness, so right now I choose to give it to you, and I ask you to please take this from me and carry it for me. So, I give it to you now, in Jesus' name. Amen."

When we were finished I asked the Lord if there was anything that He wanted this man to know. The man said he had no thoughts come to his mind, but when I asked him how he felt when he thought about his friend being in hell he said, "At ease; peace." He then said, "It was his choice; whether he is in heaven or hell shouldn't be my burden." Those two thoughts came from the Lord and brought peace to his heart. The Lord took his grief and his sadness from him and gave him the insight that it was his friend's choice and that he shouldn't carry that burden. The truth set him free from his worry and sadness about his friend. I didn't know what to say to comfort him, but the Lord did and took away his sadness.

Sadness over Loss of Father Prior to Birth

I saw a woman who had a history of alcohol abuse and depression and had experienced a great deal of trauma, abuse, and loss in her lifetime. She had been sober for three months, but was fighting the urge to drink after a recent relationship breakup. In order to begin the ministry process I asked her what was the most traumatic loss she had experienced. To my surprise she told me that the death of her father prior to her birth was the greatest loss for her and created the greatest emotional pain for her. It is not uncommon for individuals to grow up without a parent like this, but it is surprising to have someone say it was their greatest loss.

I asked this woman how she felt when she thought about her biological father whom she had never met, and she told me she felt lonely and sad. She said she felt sad because she never got to know him, he was murdered and his murderer was never convicted, and she wished that she knew the truth about his death. She also said that she was sad because she believes her life would have been very different if she had grown up with him, because she had always felt alone and had had to fight for herself with no one to defend her or protect her. I had never seen someone who was so emotional about the loss of someone prior to their birth, but I led her in a prayer to tell the Lord why she was so sad about the loss of her father and to give her sadness to Him. After we prayed I asked her how she felt and she said, "Sad, but better." She said she felt better but still felt some sadness because she did not know the truth about the death of her father. I led her in another prayer saying, "Lord, it makes me sad that I do not know how my father died. But Lord, I am tired of carrying this sadness, so right now I choose to give it to You and ask You to carry it for me. In Jesus' name I pray."

I then prayed and asked the Lord to carry her sadness for her and replace it with His peace. I also asked the Lord if there was anything that He wanted her to know. Immediately, she opened her eyes and said, "Let it go; put it in His hands." I asked her how she felt and she said she felt "blank." Then she said, "I felt a lot of pressure lifted off. My heart is not heavy like it was! I feel peace. That's awesome!" I asked her if there was any more sadness or any negative feelings and she said, "It's all good; it's all clear. No more sadness; I feel happy! I'm smiling. There's no more sadness in my heart anymore! That's awesome! Wow! I've prayed and prayed for relief and never got any till now. My heart is fuzzy with joy! It's like God just took the heaviness off my head and just pulled it off! I can feel the Holy Spirit all over me; look at the hair on my arm-- it's standing up! Wow!"

What an amazing thing it is to witness such powerful demonstrations of emotion-healing prayer and to see the Lord set captives free. Each time I witness such experiences it makes me more excited about Jesus and I feel full of the Holy Spirit also. This was just the beginning of the journey to freedom for this woman, but it proved to her that the Lord can do for her what no counselor, psychiatrist or medications can do; He can give her His peace and set her free from emotional bondage. The Lord is, indeed, awesome, and wants us all to experience His perfect peace.

Sadness over the Thought of Dying

A woman came to me who had received much healing previously but who had become very fearful of dying and leaving her three children motherless. She was healthy and had no known medical problems, but knew a thirteen-year-old girl who had died a few weeks earlier, and this triggered off obsessive thoughts about dying and not being able to see her children grow up. I asked her if she knew anyone else who had died early like this and she said that she had lost five close relatives as a child, and that she felt some sadness about their losses. When she was fifteen years old her father had died, also, so she grew up without him and she felt sad that her children never met him. We prayed about her sadness over these losses and she gave them to the Lord and got rid of them.

Since she was feeling fearful I had difficulty deciding whether I needed to pray about her fear or sadness. She said that she first felt this fear when her kids were removed from her one time by Social Services when she was in a hospital. She panicked when she didn't know where they were taken and she was very fearful then that something terrible was going to happen to them and they would be scarred and emotionally damaged. I prayed about this fear that something terrible was going to happen and she had no thoughts come to her mind, but she said she felt more calm. She then said, "It would be terrible if I died young when my kids are so young. I don't want to miss out on seeing them grow up and see them have families of their own." It made her very sad to think about dying young and leaving her children behind so I decided to pray about her sadness. I led her in a prayer saying, "Lord, it makes me sad to think about dying young and leaving my kids without a mother. It makes me sad to think about missing out on seeing them grow up and raise their own families. But Lord, I'm tired of feeling this sadness, so right now I choose to give it to You, and I ask You to take my sadness from me."

After we finished praying this time, she said that she felt "Okay." She said that she felt no more sadness or fear, and she felt calm. I thought that her primary emotion was fear but when she did not respond to praying about her fear I looked for another emotion and prayed about her sadness. It worked; she left smiling and feeling peaceful and calm. Sometimes I run into cases that puzzle me, but as I continue praying the Lord shows me what to do and sets people free. I'm still learning. We have to discern whether we are dealing with a belief-based emotion like fear, or a fact-based emotion like sadness. When we have bad feelings we either need to give them to the Lord to carry, or we need to pray for truth. All of our negative feelings can be resolved using these two prayer principles, and when we pray for the right emotion and in the right way, He sets people free.

Sadness over a Tragic Accident

A prayer counselor prayed with a woman whose granddaughter was in a tragic car accident eleven years ago and at the age of three was left paralyzed from the neck down. The driver in the car was the child's biological mother. Two weeks after the accident, the child's mother just left, abandoning her completely. The granddaughter lived with her father for a while, but he could not provide the care she needed, so Social Services stepped in and took this child away from her father and placed her in a medical facility. The grandmother was experiencing emotional pain, but unsure of what emotion she was carrying. She just knew she had a "weight and heaviness" on her chest, and explained that she felt very sorry for her granddaughter.

The counselor asked her what she felt sorry about. She listed three things: first, not being able to bring her home; second, not being able to have legal people help her get her back home; and third, she felt sad that her granddaughter could not see her friends. The counselor led her in a prayer in which she gave the above sadness to the Lord and asked Him to carry it and replace it with His peace. She asked the Lord if there was any truth that He wanted her to know and received the message, "She'll be back with me."

The counselor asked her what she felt when she thought of her granddaughter, and she still felt sadness. They listed four more things that made her sad and she gave those to the Lord as well, as the counselor led her through another prayer and then asked her how she felt. She said with a huge smile, "Confident! Confident that she will be cared for!" She then explained that she felt lighter with each prayer. She said she still had some sadness so they began to make another list, but as she was making the list she realized she was just angry with the driver, the biological mother, for just abandoning her daughter completely. They made a list of eight resentments that she had towards the biological mother, and gave those resentments to the Lord and asked Him to carry them and to replace those resentments with His peace. She was still angry about one last thing, so they gave that resentment also to the Lord and asked Him to carry it and replace it with His peace. Before the counselor even had a chance to ask her how she felt when she thought of her granddaughter, she looked up at the counselor with the biggest smile and took a deep breath in, saying "The anger has lifted! I feel a whole lot better!" She began laughing and said, "It's in God's hands and He'll take care of everything!"

The counselor asked her if she had any negative feelings at all when she thought of her granddaughter, and she said she still had some sadness that her granddaughter was not able to move her arms and legs, she could not breathe on her own, and that she could not feed herself. She prayed again and asked the Lord to carry all the sadness that she had just listed and for Him to carry it and replace it with His peace, because she was tired of carrying it. The counselor then asked the Lord if there was any truth that He wanted her to know. With a big smile, she said, "I know that the next time I see her, I will be all right. I've held everything inside of me for so long and it's all coming out! I feel real good now," and she chuckled. "I've needed to get this out for a real long time! But it's funny, I've tried to get it out with two different pastors at two separate times... but I've never felt like this before!" She laughed some more... "I'm just so happy!"

It was, indeed, a tragic accident that happened to this innocent child at such a young age, and this is truly sad. But the Lord does not want us to be stuck in our sadness, even when we experience such tragic, sad circumstances. He wants to give us His perfect peace in every circumstance so that we are not overcome with sorrow but able to rejoice in hope.

Anticipatory Grief and Sadness

Sometimes individuals experience deep feelings of sadness about someone who is still alive but has a terminal illness. This is usually called "anticipatory grief," but I prefer to treat it as a form of sadness and encourage the individual to make a list of the things that make them sad when thinking about the person and anticipating their loss. It is helpful to have the person complete the statement, "It makes me sad to think about losing _____ and not being able to _____." Make a list with them of everything that is special about the person who is dying and then say a prayer and ask the Lord to take their sadness from them and carry it for them. Once they have thoroughly identified what makes them sad and they release it to the Lord, they will feel peace in their heart and not be so overwhelmed with sadness.

Sadness apart from Grief

Sadness is experienced by many people even when they have not experienced a loss, so it is very helpful to learn to identify and release sadness. Many parents, including Christian parents, experience sadness with regard to their children as a result of their personal struggles with life challenges, as a result of poor choices they make that lead to suffering, and as a result of tragic things that happen to them.

One Christian woman asked for prayer about her sadness over her daughter's life choices and rejection of her. Her daughter was abusing drugs, living with a drug-abusing boyfriend, exposing her children to the boyfriend's poor role modeling, and had cut off her mother from contact with her grandchildren. We made a list of the reasons for her sadness and prayed and gave this sadness to the Lord. When I asked her how she felt she told me that she felt peaceful and calm, even when thinking about her wayward daughter. Over a year later she continues to comment about how much peace she has about her daughter, in spite of her continuing rebellion and waywardness.

I have occasionally awakened at two in the morning and found myself thinking about friends or family members and feeling a deep sadness about things they are doing. I try to forget about them and go back to sleep, but sometimes I continue to think about them repeatedly until I talk with the Lord about my sadness and tell Him the reasons for my sadness. When I finally give my sadness to the Lord and ask Him to take it and carry it for me, it suddenly disappears and I experience peace so that I am able to go back to sleep. This is what king David appears to be describing in Psalm 3:4-5 when he wrote, "I was crying to the Lord with my voice, and He answered me from His holy mountain. I lay down and slept; I awoke, for the Lord sustains me." We all need to learn to be in constant communion with the Lord, and learn to cast all our cares upon Him so that we are able to sleep well and enjoy His peace.

Discussion Questions

1. Have you ever experienced some sadness in connection with a loss? What was it about the loss that made you feel sad?

2. What do you understand to be the difference between grief and sadness, and how can you tell them apart?

3. Have you ever prayed in this way about some sadness and seen it leave? Would you be willing to share this experience with the other class members?

4. Do you have any sadness now as you think about people you have lost? What is the reason for your sadness, and would you like to get rid of it now?

5. Can you think of a time when you experienced some deep sadness in your life that was not connected to a loss and you could not get it to leave for a while?

6. Do you have any sadness now that you would like to release through prayer?

Personal Application

Think about all of the losses that you have experienced in your life and try to identify any remaining sadness that you feel about those experiences. Write out a list of everything that makes you sad about each loss, and give your sadness to the Lord and ask Him to take it from you and carry it for you. Write down how you feel afterwards.

Also, think about anything else that you are experiencing in your life that is bringing some sadness to you. Write out the reasons for your sadness, pray and give your sadness to the Lord, and then write down how you feel after praying. Share this experience with the other class members so they can learn from your experience, and make it your goal to release any sadness that you feel in the future as soon as you experience it. Make Psalm 3:4-5 one of your prayer goals for your life and teach your family members how to practice this, as well.

CHAPTER 5

How to Overcome Anger

G rief is sometimes accompanied by other negative feelings, and when this occurs these other emotions need to be resolved in order for the person to experience complete peace from the loss. In the last chapter we talked about sadness and how to overcome it using the same principle and the same two steps as used in overcoming feelings of grief. The other two main emotions that are most commonly found to be connected to grief are anger and shame, and in this chapter we will focus on feelings of anger and how to overcome them.

I often find individuals who grieve over the loss of a loved one, but who also have feelings of anger towards them, especially when the deceased person was emotionally or physically abusive to the grieving person at times. I saw a woman who lost her father, and she felt grief over his loss. She told me how good he was to her children, how she missed having get-togethers at his house, playing horseshoes with him, playing cards with him, and taking care of him and listening to him "cutting up"

HOW TO OVERCOME ANGER

and joking around with others. She also felt sad because he suffered a great deal before dying from leukemia, and he lost his mind before he died and said some hateful things to her. This woman took care of her father for nine months before he died, and she enjoyed taking care of him and was able to make peace with him during this time. We prayed about her grief and sadness and she gave it to the Lord and asked Him to carry it for her. Afterwards she said that she felt peaceful.

Although this woman loved her father and missed him, she also had a lot of unresolved anger toward him. She stated that he was a really good man before she was six years old, but then he had a mental breakdown and began to physically and sexually abuse her for the next six years of her life. She said that he whipped her and her older brother with switches and boards, he showed favoritism to their younger siblings, he sneaked into her bedroom at night and touched her inappropriately, he blamed her for everything that went wrong in the home, and he kicked her one time when she argued with him about something. We prayed about her anger, and she gave it to the Lord and was able to completely release it. When we finished, she told me that she felt no more anger toward him and she felt very "peaceful." Once she resolved her grief, sadness and anger she had no more negative feelings while thinking about her father

Overcoming Anger

After I initially learned these simple prayer principles, I began counseling a young man in a group home who told me that he had an anger problem. He was a nice young man who was more mature than most of the other boys in the home, and he followed the rules and had a good attitude, but I was counseling him once per week and he told me that he had a problem with anger. I asked him when was the last time he got real angry so I could see how his anger was a problem. He told me, "last weekend I got mad when one of the other boys here said something to me, and I got in his face and was ready to punch him. The staff rushed over and separated us but I was so mad that I couldn't calm down; it took me thirty minutes to calm down. Then it happened again the next day when another boy said something to me that made me mad, and I got in his face and was ready to punch him. The staff rushed over and intervened and it took me another thirty minutes to calm down. Then I began to get angry at the staff for interfering. I've been angry all week at everybody!"

"Okay," I said. "Do you want help with your anger?" He said that he did, so I said, "Let me ask you this: when is the first time that you can remember getting really angry?"

Without any hesitation he immediately replied, "When I was eight years old." "What happened when you were eight years old to make you angry?" I asked.

He said, "My parents were divorced and all of us kids lived with mom. Sometimes she would take me and my little brother over to our dad's house and drop us off and we would hang around with him and play. Then she would come back and get us and take us home. One day, when I was eight years old, she took me and my little brother over to dad's house and she said, 'I'm going down to the store on the corner to get some cigarettes and then I'll come back to get you.' She took off and we began playing."

"After a while," he said, "we wondered what was taking mom so long and we stopped playing to see if she was there. She wasn't so we continued playing and every now and then we would stop again and look for her. We continued doing this until it started getting dark, and at some point I realized that she was not coming back for us. I haven't seen her or heard from her since that day. I was so mad at her that I stayed mad for two solid years. I didn't care about anything; I didn't care about school so I started skipping school, I started getting into a lot of fights, and I began using drugs and alcohol because I was so angry."

"Well, I don't blame you for being angry," I replied. "I would be angry, too, if my mother did that to me. There's nothing wrong with you for being angry; that's just normal when someone wrongs you like this. But that was nine years ago. Do you want to stay angry?"

"No, I'm tired of being angry," he said. "It gets me into trouble all the time."

"Well, I can show you how to get rid of it," I responded. "There are basically two things that you need to do to get rid of your anger. First, you have to be completely honest about your anger and write out a list of what you resent about your mother."

"Well, she was a pretty good mother before this happened," the young man said. "But it makes me mad that she lied to me, it makes me mad that she abandoned me, and it makes me mad that she has never even called me for the last nine years."

"Okay, that's a good honest list," I said, "and that's the first step in releasing it. The second step is to say a simple prayer and tell the Lord what you resent about your mother, and ask Him to take your anger from you and carry it for you. Would you be willing to try that?"

"Sure," he replied. "I'm not a religious person but I do believe in God and in prayer. I'm willing to try it."

I led this young man in a prayer and he told the Lord that he was angry at his mother for lying to him, for abandoning him, and for not contacting him for the last nine years. Then he prayed, "Lord, I'm tired of carrying this anger, so right now I choose to give it to You, and I ask You to please take it from me and carry it for me. I pray this in Jesus' name. Amen."

When we were finished with this prayer I instructed him to think about his mother and tell me how he felt. He sat there pensively for a short while, then said, "I don't feel anything; I feel calm."

"That's good," I responded. "Now I want you to think about that day when your mother lied to you and abandoned you. Think about that and tell me how you feel."

He sat there thinking about his mother and finally said, "You know, when I prayed that prayer I felt like a load was lifted from me. I don't feel anything now; I don't feel angry anymore." Then after a brief hesitation he added, "You know, I haven't seen my mother for nine years. I'd like to see her again."

I was stunned and shocked, because I didn't expect him to be ready to see his mother so soon after our prayer, but I said to him, "I know that you're going home this weekend to see your father. Why don't you talk with him and see if he could arrange for you to see your mother again?"

This young man went home that weekend and told his father that he'd like to see his mother again, and his father was also completely shocked. But when the young man returned to the group home he was changed. He no longer had that explosive anger anymore. He just had normal anger, and would get angry about something but then five minutes later it was gone and he was okay. He didn't want to hurt anyone or do any harm. He just had normal anger that did not take over and control him for hours, after he went to the root of his anger and released it.

This youth was fortunate that his anger was rooted in one memory toward one person so that he could resolve his anger by dealing with his anger toward his mother. Other people with anger problems are not so fortunate; they often have a dozen people who have wronged them or hurt them, and in such cases they need to go through this process with each one of them to get rid of their anger.

Steps for Releasing Anger

The steps for releasing anger are identical to the steps for releasing grief, except that you have to be honest about your resentments toward the individual rather than listing the things you miss about them. The following are the three steps for overcoming anger:

STEP ONE: Be completely honest about your anger.
Be completely honest about the reasons for your anger toward someone, by making a list of everything you resent or dislike about them.

STEP TWO: Ask the Lord to take your anger from you.
Tell the Lord all your resentments toward the person and then ask Him to take your anger from you and carry it for you.

STEP THREE: Repeat this process with others who have harmed you.
Make a list of everyone else who has significantly harmed you and repeat this process for each one of them.

The first two of these steps are identical to the steps for releasing grief, but anger is often cumulative so it is necessary to identify all sources of anger and eliminate them in order to eliminate an individual's anger. Once this anger is all eliminated it makes a tremendous difference in the person's life and they are able to deal with life issues without exploding or overreacting to others.

The Right to be Angry

The Bible is very clear that we should not harbor anger and resentment. In Ephesians 4:31-32 the apostle Paul said, "Let all bitterness and wrath and anger and clamor and slander be put away from you, along with all malice. And be kind to one another, tender-hearted, forgiving each other, just as God in Christ also has forgiven you." James, the half-brother of Jesus, instructed us in James 1:19-20, "But let everyone be quick to hear, slow to speak *and* slow to anger; for the anger of man does not achieve the righteousness of God."

Based upon such passages some Christians teach that we should never be angry and it is wrong to be angry, even though Jesus was angry on several occasions. In John 2:13-17 and Matthew 21:12-13 there is the famous passage about the clearing of the temple when Jesus began overturning tables and threw out the money-changers from the temple because they were making His Father's house a "den of thieves." It seems obvious that He was angry with a righteous anger and that He committed no sin, but some Christians even deny that He was angry in this instance because the Scriptures do not explicitly state here that he was angry. However, in Mark 3:5 the Scriptures state, "after looking around at them with anger, grieved at their hardness of heart, He said to the man, 'Stretch out your hand.' And he stretched it out, and his hand was restored." Jesus was righteously angry at these religious leaders for their hardness of heart and their lack of compassion for this needy man. They should have rejoiced at his healing and at the power of God, but they were so hard-hearted that it angered Jesus.

In Ephesians 4:26-27 Paul gives us the clearest statement about anger to help us understand it. He says, "Be angry, and yet do not sin; do not let the sun go down on your anger, and do not give the devil an opportunity." The first part of this verse is a quote from Psalm 4:4 where the Psalmist, David, said, "Tremble [with fear or anger], and do not sin; Meditate in your heart upon your bed, and be still." Paul and King David are both affirming here that it is not a sin to be angry, but it can lead to sin. That is why Paul goes on to say "do not let the sun go down on your anger, and do not give the devil an opportunity." When we hold onto anger it leads to sin and it gives the devil an opportunity in our lives. In Ephesians 4:30 Paul appears to be saying that our anger can "grieve the

Holy Spirit," so that is why he then said in verse 31 to "Let all bitterness and wrath and anger...be put away from you."

It is not wrong to be angry, but it is wrong to hold onto it and it will invariably lead to sin, grieve the Holy Spirit, and give the devil an opportunity in our lives. When someone has been brutally abused, it is harmful to tell them immediately that they should not be angry. Anger is a natural reaction and it is okay to be angry, so telling someone that they need to forgive, without first allowing them to ventilate and feel understood, generally leads them to respond defensively and can lead to bitterness. When I speak with people who have been abused, the first thing that I say to them is "You have a right to be angry. If I was in your shoes I would be angry, too." This is important to say so that they understand that you are not condemning them and that you are human. Once they register this information they usually relax and breathe deeply, and this is often visible. Then I go on to say, as I did with this teenager, "That was nine years ago; do you want to hang onto that anger?" Or I will ask them, "If you could get rid of your anger would you like to?"

The Impact of Anger

When Paul says, "do not let the sun go down on your anger, and do not give the devil an opportunity" (Ephesians 4:26-27) he is saying something very important. He is clearly indicating that things from our past can and do control us, so we have to deal with those past events. From my 35 years of clinical experience I am convinced that over 90% of all Christians have a lot of anger in their lives from past hurts and offenses that continue to affect them in their daily lives.

The importance of releasing our anger is underscored by Paul's comments in Galatians 5:19-21 where he provides a list of fifteen "deeds of the flesh" which he contrasts with the "fruit of the Spirit." In the middle of his list of fifteen "deeds of the flesh" he includes, "enmities, strife, jealousy, outbursts of anger, disputes, dissensions, factions," each of which is a direct manifestation of anger. This means that almost half of these fleshly behaviors are the result of holding on to anger. We cannot afford to hold on to our anger, because when we do we are unable to "walk by the Spirit" (v. 16), or be "led by the Spirit" (v. 18), and Paul says that "the flesh sets its desire against the Spirit, and the Spirit against the flesh; for these are in opposition to one another, so that you may not do the things that you please" (Galatians 5:17).

Anger is one of the primary underlying causes of mental health problems. Some of the mental health disorders that are rooted in anger are conduct disorder, oppositional defiant disorder, antisocial personality disorder, intermittent explosive disorder, bipolar disorder, substance abuse disorders, and marital problems. It is impossible to help people overcome these disorders without helping them overcome their anger.

Manifestations of Anger

Our churches are full of anger, and many Christians have a problem with anger but they deny it. There was a man who occasionally was invited to lead worship at the church I attended who was a very skilled musician with a beautiful voice. His worship songs were uplifting to most people except for a few in the church who knew that he had a serious problem with his anger. On his job site he sometimes became so angry that he screamed and shouted profanity at others in fits of rage. Some of his fellow-Christians who worked with him tried to talk with him about his anger and to offer him help but he never accepted it or received any help. He continues to throw fits of rage at work, and to lead worship in the church when he has the opportunity.

Other Christians have less of a problem with their anger, but they nonetheless have a problem with it. I know a Christian man who is always very pleasant at church and smiles all the time. He seems like the most pleasant man, but his wife states that he was always so critical of their children that they did not like to be around him and avoided him. He also criticizes and complains continually about his wife for little things, and this throws her into depression from time to time. I have no doubt that this critical spirit is rooted in feelings of anger toward his own father who was always very critical and disapproving of him. He speaks highly of his father, but admits that he dislikes being around him and seldom visits him even though he lives nearby. After being at his father's house for fifteen minutes he becomes anxious about leaving. He has a problem with anger that has damaged his family.

Forty Years of Anger

A man came with a friend of his to a weekly Set Free meeting one time to observe. During this meeting I explained how the Lord is able to take our anger and grief and carry it for us. Then I asked if anyone had some anger or grief that they wanted to pray about, and a young man sitting next to me volunteered. He stated that he was very angry at his father who had been very abusive to him, and as he began talking about the reasons for his anger I began writing them down and making a list. I prayed through this list with the young man, and when he was done, his anger toward his father was gone and he stated that he felt no more anger or hostility toward him.

The visitor said nothing during the meeting but thanked me afterwards for the demonstration. The following week he came to my office and told me that he was so impacted by the meeting that he went home and spent the entire weekend on his knees giving anger to the

Lord that he had carried for 40 years. He said that he had studied the Bible intensely for 40 years, he memorized it, meditated on it, confessed his sins repeatedly, and spoke to every pastor he knew in an effort to find freedom from his anger, but nothing had worked. But after thoroughly admitting the reasons for his anger and giving it to the Lord he felt completely released from the 40 years of anger.

This man told me that he had been through many counseling sessions with a Christian counselor in an effort to release his anger and save his marriage and it failed, but after one hour of observing a prayer session he was able to find freedom. He became passionate about this prayer ministry and began sharing it with his friends, family, and pastor. He had been bitter toward his pastor and the church for their failure to help him, but after being set free he returned to church and began to experience the joy of the Lord again. He continues to serve the Lord and to try to spread the good news about Jesus and His power to set captives free.

Youth Worker Releases Anger

A youth worker told how he first learned to use these prayer principles on himself. He was taking a group of students to a concert one day and one boy came who had a cold and sat in the front seat next to the youth minister. The boy began coughing without covering his mouth and the youth minister told him that he should stay home if he was sick, but he insisted that he was okay. However, he kept coughing and the youth minister kept telling him to cover his mouth but the youth did not, and the minister could feel himself being hit in the face with this boy's spittle. He was very irritated and angry at this youth, but when he woke up the next morning sick he was furious. He was so angry at the young man that he couldn't think about him without feeling rage, and he knew he could not afford to hold onto this anger and be able to minister to him.

Then he thought about my book, which he had read previously, and decided to try to give his anger to the Lord. He made a list of the reasons for his anger and then he prayed and asked the Lord to take it from him, and he was amazed at how quickly his anger disappeared.

This youth worker's wife had told him that she had been sexually abused one time by a man in her hometown, and he was never punished for this. It made him angry to think about this man who had so mistreated her but he didn't know the man and had never met him. Then one day he had to make a trip to that town and he began to visualize what he would do if he saw this man. He was so angry that while packing his clothes he packed a gun in his suitcase in case he ran into the man. He knew that it was wrong for him to harbor such anger and that as a pastor he should set an example for others in his church, but he was so consumed with anger that he wanted to hurt the man who had hurt his wife. Fortunately, before he left for the trip he fell under conviction and talked with the Lord about his anger and asked Him to take it from him. Immediately upon praying, his heart softened and his anger faded. He no longer felt ill-will toward the man, even though he knew that the man had never received any consequence for the harm he had done to his wife years earlier. The Lord took his anger from him and replaced it with peace so that he could leave it to the Lord to bring consequences in the right time and manner.

Anger Management

Whenever sensational acts of violence occur, the media begin interviewing professionals who recommend better gun control and more mental health services. Unfortunately, they do not disclose the fact that most of those who commit these acts of violence are already taking psychotropic medications and that their acts of violence are medication induced.

Adam Lanza who entered Sandy Hook Elementary School on December 14, 2012 and killed 20 children and 6 adults, was under the care of a psychiatrist already and taking an antidepressants which are known to have the ability to cause acts of violence. However, Adam Lanza's medical records were not released by the state of Connecticut out of fear by the Attorney General that others who are taking antidepressants would quit taking their medications (Watson 2013). The other major solution offered by mental health professionals to control violence and anger in addition to medication is anger management. Anger management classes have gained wide publicity, and courts all across the country use them as a first and last resort for dealing with domestic violence and for criminal acts of violence. However, the research on the effectiveness of anger management is not very impressive.

A case in point is professional basketball player Ron Artest, who was playing for the Indiana Pacers in 2002, when he assaulted his girlfriend repeatedly and was ordered by the court to go to anger management classes. However, he had anger problems since childhood and had been to many anger management classes previously. In spite of his completion of another set of anger management classes he was involved in a fight during a nationally-televised NBA game in 2004 when a fan threw something at him and he went into the stands to fight the individual and a massive brawl erupted in the arena.

Ron Artest was ordered to complete anger management again. He began regular therapy sessions with a prominent therapist and received the best anger management treatment that money can buy. After completing these therapy sessions he decided to change his name in order to change his image, and he became legally known as "Metta World Peace." Then in 2012 while playing the Oklahoma City Thunder he became excited after dunking the ball and began bouncing around and beating on his chest and flailing his arms around, when he hit one of the Oklahoma

Thunder players with his elbow and knocked him out, giving him a concussion. It may not have been intentional but he never stopped to help the injured player or apologize. Mr. World Peace apparently still has an anger problem after all of the therapy and anger management he has been through during his entire life, since age 8 (Edelson, 2004).

One of the preeminent researchers of anger management is Dr. Ray DiGiuseppe, who told one reporter, "Anger management classes, I think, are a Band-Aid; they allow people to feel they've done something but they haven't had any kind of real treatment" (Carey, 2004). In 2003 Dr. DiGiuseppe conducted a review of 92 anger-management treatments which included more than 1800 subjects, and he concluded that the classes can reduce feelings of anger a little in people who are motivated to change (Carey, Benedict 2004). Many of the anger-management studies are done with college students, but studies done with criminals and those known to have serious anger problems consistently fail to show a significant impact. In a review of 22 studies of state programs, a team of psychologists in Texas and New York reported that the courses had little positive effect upon the subjects' anger (Carey, 2004). The bottom line is, there is no evidence that anger management has a significant impact upon the anger of those with serious anger-control issues, but it is the best that mental health professionals have to offer.

Atheist Released from Anger

Not only are our churches full of anger, but our whole society is full of anger. I go to the local jail each week and talk with the men and women in the jails about how to be set free from their anger. I find, of course, that our jails are full of angry people, many of whom have already completed anger management classes, and very few of whom ever say that it helped them. One day I was in the jail talking to a group of about twelve inmates about anger. I asked them how many of them had an anger problem and almost all of them admitted that they did. I asked them how many of them had completed anger management, and about 80% of them had. Then, I asked them how many of them found anger management helpful, and none of them said it was.

A young man standing to my right spoke up and said, "I know that I have an anger problem, but the problem is that I'm an atheist."

"That's okay," I responded. "Have you been to anger management?" He said that he had been to it four times, and he was only nineteen years old. "Well, let me ask you this. If I could show you how to get rid of your anger through prayer would you consider that there is a God?" He smiled slightly and shrugged his shoulders, as if to say, "Maybe."

Several days later I was leaving the jail when I saw this same young man waving at me from another cell and trying to get my attention. I went to his cell and asked the officer to open the door so I could visit with him. When the door was opened I asked him, "Would you like to try to get rid of that anger?"

"Yes, I would," he answered.

"So, who are you angry at?" I asked. "I'm angry at my grandpa," he said. I asked him, "Why are you so angry at your grandpa?"

This young man began to tell me about his grandfather and how abusive he had been to him. He told me that his grandfather held him down one time and let his brother beat him up. He told me about more abuse until we had a list of seven resentments he had towards his grandfather. When he was finished I explained that he had taken the first step to releasing his anger by just being completely honest about the reasons for his anger. Then I told him the second step was to sincerely say a simple prayer, telling God why he was angry, and asking Him to take it from him. I asked him if he was willing to do this and he said he was.

I led this young man in a prayer and he told the Lord each resentment he had toward his grandfather, and then said, "Lord, I'm tired of carrying this anger and hatred so right now I choose to give it to You, and I ask You to please take it from me. I pray this in Jesus' name. Amen."

When he finished praying I asked him to think about his grandfather and tell me how he felt toward him. He stood there thinking for a while and said nothing so I asked him again, "How do you feel when you think about your grandfather?" He said, "I don't feel anything." I told him to keep thinking about him and about all his abuse and then tell me how he felt. After another brief period of reflection he finally said again, "I don't feel anything."

"You mean to tell me that five minutes ago you were angry and hated your grandpa and now you don't feel any anger toward him?" He nodded in agreement. "So, where did your anger go?" I asked. He looked me in the eyes and just pointed up with his finger. "Do you think there might be a God?" I asked. He nodded at me and said, "Yes."

The next day I went back to the jail with a friend and we got this young man out of his cell and sat across a table from him. "How is your anger today?" I asked.

"I don't have any anger," he replied.

"So, what do you think about that?" I asked him.

"I think it's amazing!"

"Let me ask you a question," I said. "If you could be 100% sure that you're going to heaven when you die, would you want to?" He said that he would, so I told my friend to tell him how to be sure he is going to heaven, and my friend shared the gospel with him and he received Jesus as his Savior.

One day he was an atheist, but once the Lord took his anger from him after his many attempts to overcome his anger on his own, he witnessed the power of God and the goodness of God and his heart softened to Him.

The Lord Jesus did miracles for people who were unbelievers and it often led them to follow Him. The same thing can happen for us today as we use the power of prayer to supernaturally help set captives free from their grief, anger, and emotional problems.

Helpful Guidelines

When helping others release their anger there are several guidelines that I have found to be helpful. First, it is helpful to affirm their right to be angry. It has been discussed earlier in this chapter that it helps individuals to hear, what they intuitively understand, that anger is normal and okay. There is nothing wrong with feeling anger. I like to share Ephesians 4:26-27 with them that first says, "Be angry." I like to tell clients, "It's okay to be angry and you have a right to be angry. If I was in your place I'd be angry, too." When we hear about a violent crime, the sexual abuse of a child, or some other vicious act, it is normal to feel anger, and we should be angry. That is not wrong, but our anger can lead us to overreact to others and lead to sinful actions if we hold on to it for long. It is helpful to tell the client, "There is nothing wrong with being angry. It is a normal reaction to wrong things that happen."

The second thing that I like to tell clients with anger is to warn them of the dangers of remaining angry for long. I like to say, "The Bible says, 'Be angry and yet do not sin; do not let the sun go down on your anger.'" I explain to them that this literally means that we should not hold onto our anger overnight. Our anger is not wrong, but the longer we hang onto it the greater the likelihood is that we will act out in anger and do or say something that we will regret or that will lead us into sin.

Finally, I like to confront them with a choice by asking, "If you could get rid of your anger would you like to?" Most people when approached in this way say that they would like to get rid of their anger. If they say they want to, then you can simply share with them the two steps to freedom from anger, or share a personal anecdote from your own life about how you were able to release your anger. If they are willing, help them make up a list of the reasons for their anger toward someone, and lead them in a prayer to release their anger. Afterwards, ask them how they feel and ask them to rate their anger on a 10-point scale. If their anger is gone, they will be encouraged, and you can talk with them about the power of prayer and encourage them to continue to pray to find complete freedom in their lives.

When Someone Does Not Want to Release Their Anger

When asked, most people say that they would like to get rid of their anger, but about five percent of the time they say they do not. When this happens there is always an underlying lie that they believe that prevents them from releasing their anger. Sometimes they believe that the person will get away without punishment or consequence, and they feel it is their responsibility to hold them accountable. At other times people believe that they will be hurt again if they release their anger and let down their guard. They believe that they cannot protect themselves if they are not angry.

When the person believes such lies it sometimes helps to ask them what they believe will happen if they release their anger, and then help them articulate their thinking. If they give permission, you can pray with them and ask the Lord what He wants them to know about their belief that it is their responsibility to punish the person, or their belief that they will be hurt again if they release their anger. Instruct them to be quiet, and record any comments they make. When they are willing to listen to the Lord, He will speak truth into their minds to remove the false belief that is holding their anger in place. If this happens, you can then make a list of the reasons for their anger and ask the Lord to carry it for them.

Radical Transformation

The Lord is in the business of setting captives free and He loves to radically transform lives to show His power. The world does not know how to solve the problem of violence or how to resolve anger in people's lives, but the Lord can set us free from our anger through this simple prayer process. This is not difficult; any Christian can learn to do this and help themselves, their friends, and their fellow Christians to release their anger.

Imagine the impact it would have if Christians from all dominations began to use this simple process to release their anger and the world began to see that churches were setting people free from their anger in a way that they cannot. The Lord would be glorified, Christians would be radically transformed, and people would be drawn to the Lord and to churches for help and healing. May God spread this message to believers all across the nation and around the world, so that the Lord will be magnified.

Discussion Questions

1. When you think about people you have lost, did you have any anger connected to these losses? Share this with your group.

2. Does it make sense to you biblically that people have a right to be angry?

3. Do you believe that Dr. Gardner is correct in his statement that churches are full of angry people, and that over 90% of church members have unresolved feelings of anger?

4. Think of one person toward whom you have some anger. Would you like to get rid of this anger, if possible?

5. What do you think would happen if everyone in your church eliminated all their anger? What difference do you think it would make in their lives and in the church?

6. If there is anyone toward whom you have anger and you do not want to release your anger, write down the reason for your reluctance to release it. What do you think would happen if you released it? Pray and ask the Lord what He wants you to know about your belief that you need to hold onto your anger.

Personal Application

Think about all of the losses that you have experienced in your lifetime and try to identify any remaining feelings of anger that you have that are related to them. Write out a list of everything that makes you angry about each loss and give your anger to the Lord and ask Him to take it from you and carry it for you. Write down how you feel afterwards.

Consider, also, any other anger that you are carrying at this time, no matter how small it is. Select one person toward whom you have some anger, write out all the resentments you have towards them and everything about them that irritates you, then give your anger to the

Lord and ask Him to take it and carry it for you. Share this experience with your class so that they can learn from your experience, and make it your goal to release all anger that you experience in the future as soon as you experience it.

CHAPTER 6

Overcoming
Anger at God

worked at a state prison for several years, left that job for another opportunity, and then a year later I decided to return to the prison job. My former boss was gone and a new clinical supervisor interviewed me and hired me to go back to my former position. On my first day back at work he told me that one of the prison staff had told him that I was "overly Christian," and he said that I would not be allowed to talk with any inmates about spiritual things. I reasoned with him, but he was firm in his decision and insisted that I must not talk with inmates about God or anything spiritual.

If I had been told this before being hired I would probably have declined the job, but now that I was hired and had no other source of income, I reluctantly consented to this rule. I performed my job duties and steered clear of any spiritual or religious topics for a period of time and built my relationship with this new boss. Then one day I was talking with an inmate who was discussing his background and he told me that when he was a child his father died and he became very angry at God, and his anger became a driving force in his life that led to rebellion, drug abuse, and criminal behavior. I wondered how I was going to help this young man with his emotional issues without discussing God.

I spoke with my supervisor and explained the situation and asked him how he wanted me to deal with this inmate. He had developed confidence in my integrity and professionalism by this point and agreed that this issue needed to be discussed. He agreed that it was impossible to avoid talking with this man about these spiritual issues and he gave me permission to talk with the inmate about his anger toward God. From that point on I was given full freedom to use my discretion in talking about spiritual matters with inmates. Clearly, anger toward God was a significant issue that needed to be addressed.

Anger: A fact-based Emotion

In Chapter Three I described anger as a "fact-based" emotion to distinguish it from the group of "belief-based" emotions. This distinction is important because it determines the process by which anger can be removed. Jesus was angry on a number of occasions, but His anger was not based upon lies He believed or distorted thinking; as the Son of God it was impossible for Him to have any distorted thinking. No, His anger was based upon His righteous anger at sin and at witnessing the gross evil and callousness of men.

Individuals who have been physically or sexually abused are also righteously angry at the perpetrators of their abuse and there is no sin in their feelings of anger, but they often violate the Scriptural commands to "not let the sun go down on [their] anger" (Ephesians 4:26) and to put aside "all bitterness and wrath and anger and clamor and slander" (Ephesians 4:31). However, most people do not know how to release their anger. Many people have tried to forgive their abusers but still have some anger in spite of their efforts and prayers to forgive their "trespassers." When told that they have a right to be angry and asked if they would like to get rid of their anger, most people want to do so; they just need some instruction to know how to do this.

However, many people are also angry at God for things that He allows to happen in their lives. I never tell such people that they have a right to be angry at God, because they don't, but I sometimes tell them "I don't blame you for being angry; we all get angry at God at times." I never justify someone's anger at God; anger at God is never justifiable, because He is always good, but as a fellow-human with limited foresight and understanding I acknowledge that sometimes it is very difficult to understand why God allows certain things to happen.

A Pastor Angry at God

I know of several pastors who have admitted that they went through a period of time when they were angry at God. When a pastor is angry at God it makes it very difficult for them to preach sermons from week to week. One pastor came for help who admitted that he was angry with God and didn't know how to overcome it. He told me about about a series of events that happened in his life as a child that had profoundly affected him then, and were still bothering him. He told me that when he was nine years old his father was involved in a car accident and was hospitalized for a long time. He worried about losing his father and being left alone and he prayed for him. While in the hospital his father told him to take care of his mother if he died, then had a heart attack and died. This boy had been very close to his father, and had spent a lot of time with him talking, riding around with him, and working on projects together. His father was very calm, joked around with him, and gave him good spiritual counsel. After this tragic death the pastor felt very alone, and his mother began to drink so she was not able to provide him the guidance he needed. She began dating other men and worked all the time, leaving this boy alone a lot. He became rebellious, and then when he was twelve years old his mother also died in a car accident.

This man said that his father was a good, honest man and he needed his father. It made him angry at God for taking his father away, and then taking his mother away also. I asked him to tell me what else made him angry at God. He said that God seemed so distant from him and he received no direction when it was needed. God allowed him to go through all these painful experiences that were so unnecessary, and he needed his father. This boy had no other male father-figure or mentor to replace his father as a child. He had no one to talk to and he felt ignored. He knew that God promised to be a "father to the fatherless," but he never felt the presence of God in his life.

After this pastor stated the reasons for his anger, I led him in a prayer and he told the Lord why he was angry and then gave his anger to the Lord and asked Him to carry it for him. I prayed and asked the Lord what he wanted the pastor to know, and the following thoughts came to his mind: "I love you; I chose you." I asked him how that made him feel and he told me that he felt peaceful and calm and had no more anger toward God. We then talked about his father and what he missed about him, and made a list of fifteen things he remembered about his father that he missed. We prayed and the pastor gave his grief and sadness to the Lord, and he was able to release it all. When we were finished he was relaxed and said that he felt completely at peace about his father.

Steps for Releasing Anger toward God

The steps for releasing anger toward God are the same as for releasing anger toward anyone else, even though our anger toward God is never righteous.

STEP ONE: Be completely honest about your anger.
The first step is to be honest with God and make a list of our complaints and grievances toward the Lord.

STEP TWO: *Ask the Lord to take your anger from you.*
The second step is to pray and ask the Lord to take your anger from you and carry it for you. When you pray in this way, the Lord will take your anger from you and replace it with His peace, and along with peace He will give you insights to understand Him more.

Job: A Righteous Man Angry at God

Job is a perfect example of this in the Bible. We are told that Job was a righteous man, but Satan came into God's presence and asked permission to attack Job and afflict him, and God gave him permission to afflict Job but not to take his life. So, in one day Job, who was a wealthy man with ten children, lost a home, his children, his servants, and his livestock. Job defended God's right to take away what He had given Job, and he remained faithful to the Lord. Then Job arose and tore his robe and shaved his head, and he fell to the ground and worshiped. He said in Job 1:20-22,

> Naked I came from my mother's womb,
> And naked I shall return there.
> The LORD gave and the LORD has taken away.
> Blessed be the name of the LORD.
> Through all this Job did not sin nor did he blame God.

Satan, again, spoke to God and requested permission to afflict Job, this time with health problems, and God gave Him permission to do so. In Job 2:7-10 we read the following:

> Then Satan went out from the presence of the LORD and smote Job with sore boils from the sole of his foot to the crown of his head. And he took a potsherd to scrape himself while he was sitting among the ashes.

Then his wife said to him, Do you still hold fast your integrity? Curse God and die!" But he said to her, You speak as one of the foolish women speaks. Shall we indeed accept good from God and not accept adversity? In all this Job did not sin with his lips.

When Job's three friends came to comfort him, then Job broke down and cursed the day of his birth and began to complain about the injustice of his plight. His friends told him that God does not punish the righteous and urged him to admit and confess his sins so that God would turn away His anger from Job. These accusations made Job angry, and in Job 10:1-3 he finally began to turn his anger toward God:

> I loathe my own life; I will give full vent to my complaint;
> I will speak in the bitterness of my soul.
> I will say to God, "Do not condemn me;
> Let me know why Thou dost contend with me.
> Is it right for Thee indeed to oppress,
> To reject the labor of Thy hands,
> And to look favorably on the schemes of the wicked?"

Job was angry at God but knew it was folly to argue with God. In the end the Lord spoke to him and brought truth to him, and he repented of his arrogance toward God. Then the Lord elevated him to a position of greater affluence and blessed the latter years of his life more than the former ones. Job then interceded for his friends so that God did not curse them for their wrongful accusations and their lack of compassion for Job.

When we experience very painful things in life and cannot understand God's ways, most of us respond like Job, and become angry with the Lord. But the Lord is patient with us and He will correct our beliefs and give us truth if we are willing to honestly lay our complaints before Him and give them to Him.

Releasing Anger toward God Naturally

Sometimes anger toward God can be released naturally as an individual receives healing for other feelings, without explicitly taking them through these two steps. A woman told me that she had been depressed for eighteen years, since her mother had died. She was just a child at the time but she remembered how her mother used to play the piano, and there was one particular song that she really enjoyed. She said that her mother was a wonderful mother, she never raised her voice, and she was very loving and affectionate. This woman missed seeing her mother's pretty blue eyes, her crooked smile, going to church with her, and hearing her pray. She also missed looking for rocks and crystals with her, snuggling with her when she was sick, taking naps with her, helping her cook, and getting up early in the morning so her mother could fix her hair. We made a list of twenty-seven things that she missed about her mother, then we prayed and she gave her grief to the Lord.

She also had some sadness, and as she began talking about her mother's last days she became very tearful. She told me that her mother had cancer and she suffered, but she never showed her children that she was in pain. When her mother had to be moved to a hospital far away from home it was sad that she got to see her mother only once per month. The last time she saw her mother, her mother could not talk but she smiled at her and held her hand. When her mother died, the daughter was angry at her for leaving them and angry at God for letting her die. We identified six reasons for her sadness and she gave her sadness to the Lord and asked Him to take it from her. Then I prayed and asked the Lord what He wanted her to know.

"My mom loves me," she said. The word "sunset" came to her mind and she began remembering how she used to sit with her mother and watch the sunsets, and this brought tears of joy to her eyes. I asked her how she felt and she said, "Happy. I'm happy that I got to have her as long as I did." She said that her sadness was gone so I asked her if she still felt angry at her mother and angry at God. She said, "I miss her but I have no anger toward her or God." After carrying these feelings of grief and sadness for eighteen years she was suddenly free! She said she felt "happy and calm," and she left the room with a smile on her face. When the Lord lifted her sadness she was not only set free from her grief and sadness, but also from her anger toward God and toward her mother without specifically addressing these feelings.

Anger at God for Taking a Child

I was contacted by a man who had lost his twenty-one-year-old son a year earlier. He told me that his son lived with him and was a good kid who never got into trouble. One evening he went to bed and thirty minutes later he died from a brain aneurysm. This man was very distraught even a year after this loss. I shared with him the two steps for releasing grief, the first of which is to be completely honest about what you miss about the person. He was willing to do this, so we talked about his son and what he missed about him. We made a list of twenty things he missed about his son, and then I explained that the second step was to say a prayer and tell the Lord what he missed and ask the Lord to take his grief from him.

The father hesitated at this suggestion. I asked him if that was a problem and he told me that he wasn't talking to God; he was angry at Him for taking his son from him. I asked him if he would like to get rid of his anger and he said he would, so I asked him why he was angry at God. He told me that he was angry because there are so many worthless young people running around whom God allows to live, but He chose to take his son from him. He was also angry because his son was too young to die, and he was angry because he would never have any grandchildren. We made a list of the reasons for his anger at God, and then I led him in a prayer to tell Him why he was angry and to ask Him to take it from him. When we were finished he said he was no longer angry at God, so we then went ahead and prayed about his grief over the loss of his son, and the Lord took his grief and sadness from him. Before he was able to pray about his grief, however, he had to first release his anger toward God.

Anger at God for Legal Problems

I met a young woman in jail who said that she had a God-fearing family and had once been very close to God, but she was now in jail and was angry at God. Curious about how a person who had once been close to God had strayed so far away, I asked about her family background and criminal history. She stated that she was raised by a godly elderly woman until age three and then lived with her biological mother and stepdad during weekdays, both of whom were violent. It was this godly elderly woman who taught her about the Lord, but she experienced a lot of abuse growing up around her parents. She said that she was very close to the Lord as a teenager and loved Him very much.

At age seventeen she married her husband and remained married to him for twelve years. From this marriage she had two children. Years earlier her biological father had died, as well as an eighteen-month-old nephew and her best friend. These losses were very painful and led her to begin using drugs. A year later a neighbor woman began spanking her daughter who had accidentally knocked some clothes off her clothes line, and this woman went to defend her daughter and ended up beating the neighbor badly in front of her own children. Her protective reaction to this woman was normal, but her overreaction was probably due to the unresolved anger she had from growing up in an abusive home. As a result of this assault her children were removed from her custody, and she was sent to prison for ten months and lost everything, including permanently losing her parental rights. At this time she became very angry at God whom she felt had abandoned her.

It was very difficult talking with this woman because of her anger and her skepticism about prayer. I shared my usual stories about how the Lord is able to release us from anger and asked if she wanted to get rid of her anger. She said that she did but she did not believe this prayer process would help because she had already tried to pray about it. She said that her real problem was her anger at God. She was angry at Him for allowing her to lose her children and everything else after she had been so close to Him and tried to serve Him. She felt like her life was like a game to God. She said that she was angry at God for allowing her to be tempted by the devil the same way He had allowed Job to be tempted, just to prove to Satan that Job would be faithful to Him. This made her very angry.

She was still skeptical, but eventually agreed to talk with the Lord about her anger. I led her in a prayer in which she told the Lord why she was angry at Him and then said, "I'm tired of being angry at You, so right now I choose to give it to You, and I ask You to please take this from me and replace it with your peace." After this prayer I asked her how she felt when she thought about God. She looked perplexed and after some hesitation she finally said, "I don't feel any anger." She said that she felt some disappointment and hurt but no longer had any anger toward God. This woman had been carrying this anger toward God for years, but was released from it instantly when she prayed and gave it to God.

It's an amazing thing to see how simply God can remove anger when a person is willing to be honest with Him and give it to Him to carry. The Lord is able to release an individual instantly when they give their anger to Him.

Anger at God Due to Marriage Problems

A woman came for counseling due to marital problems she was having. She grew up in a loving home with parents who got along well and grandparents who took her to church and church camps, and she married a man whom she believed God brought to her as an answer to prayer. But when her husband's best friend died he became depressed and began drinking, and he disappeared for days at a time on drinking binges. His drinking upset this woman so much that she nit-picked at him and yelled at him in front of the children, then felt bad about her emotional outbursts. She said she was angry at her husband but was especially angry at God for allowing her to marry an alcoholic, for allowing his drinking to harm her and her children, and she felt that He was punishing her for no reason.

I led this woman in a prayer, telling God why she was angry at Him and then asking Him to take her anger from her. Then I asked the Lord if there was anything He wanted her to know. She said, "One day we may be able to help other couples; everything happens for a reason; God has a purpose; I know it will be okay; He won't hang us out to dry." I asked her how she felt and she said she no longer had any anger at God. The following week when she came to see me, she said that she had had a good week. She had gotten along much better with her husband, and felt much more peaceful. She said that he drank a little but she didn't get upset at him or nit-pick at him, and he quit after a few drinks.

With her anger at God out of the way we prayed about the loss of a close friend, and she released the things she missed about her. She prayed and told the Lord each of the nine things she missed about her friend and asked the Lord to carry them for her. Then I prayed and asked the Lord what He wanted her to know. Initially, the thoughts that came to her were, "She's at peace; she's no longer in pain; and she's having a good time." Then she had a very clear, vivid picture of her deceased friend's mother who was laughing and telling her, "Stop worrying about my daughter; she's fine." This picture that came to her mind was so vivid that she cried tears of joy saying, "It felt like she was right here with me." She said she felt peaceful when thinking about her deceased friend and said, "It's weird. I have never felt like He (God) was talking to me before!"

What a powerful demonstration of God's love and desire for His children to be set free and to experience His peace. He set her free from her anger toward Him, and then set her free from her nit-picking, her anger toward her husband, and her grief and sadness over the loss of her friend.

Anger at God Leads to Incarceration

I saw a young man in jail who had received the Lord as His Savior several months earlier and whom I saw each week when I went to the jail. After his new birth he looked much happier and assured me that he is certain that he is going to heaven when he dies. One day I asked him about his tattoos and he pointed out one tattoo of a person's name. He told me that this was a two-year-old child he knew very well who died after he had prayed fervently for her. When his prayers failed and the child died he became very angry at God. Although he was saved now and happy to be a Christian, he admitted when I inquired that he still felt some anger at God about the death of this child. I asked him if he would like to get rid of it if he could, and he said he would. I find it fascinating that people want to release their anger at God but do not know how to do it.

We sat down at a table in the cell house and I asked him why he was angry at God. He told me, "Because He allowed Erin to die." I asked for other reasons for his anger and he told me he was angry because he has been in prison for ten years, God could have guided him and kept him from this type of life; he didn't ask to be born and God let him be born and go through such painful things. He also said that it seems that God is playing games with us and showing Satan what He can do. So I led him in a prayer to tell God why he was angry. Then I prayed and asked the Lord to take this man's anger from him and I asked the Lord if there was anything He wanted this man to know. He said, "He loves me. I am picturing Him [the Lord] in white and He is saying, 'I love you, my son.'"

I asked him how that made him feel and he said that he felt calm and peaceful. He said that he felt no more anger at God. Weeks later I continued to see him and he was always smiling and happy to see me. He said that he no longer had any anger at God and he continued to read his Bible and pray regularly.

Anger at God Due to False Prophecy

A woman became angry at God because at age sixteen she lost three of the people in her life who were closest to her. She grew up with loving parents and grandparents who took her to church and provided her a stable home, but when she was sixteen years old her grandmother died suddenly, and then her grandfather died slowly. Several preachers and so-called prophets prayed for her grandfather and told her that the Lord had told them that he was going to be healed. She prayed earnestly for him but he died anyway. This made her very angry at the Lord. Then she began spending a lot of time with her uncle who died very suddenly without any warning, which intensified her anger at God.

This anger led her to begin associating with the wrong crowd and experimenting with drugs. She married a man who was not a godly man and he became abusive to her, which led her to engage in other behaviors that led her to feel guilty and shameful. When I initially spoke with her she was very tearful and anxious and was not ready to do any praying. But the next time I saw her she had been through another crisis and said, "I'm ready to do whatever I need to do." I asked her to tell me why she was angry at God and she told me how the preachers and "prophets" misled her to believe God would heal her grandfather, how she prayed for him in vain and believed her prayers would be answered, how her uncle then died after she became really close to him, and it seemed to her that God was deliberately taking away from her everyone with whom she was close.

I told her to be honest with the Lord about her anger and to ask Him to take away her anger. In her prayer she said, "Lord, I'm tired of carrying all this hatred and so I choose now to give it to you and ask you to take it from me." I prayed and asked the Lord if there was anything that He wanted her to know and she said, "I don't feel angry; I just feel shameful because He has done so much good for me; I have two wonderful kids and a good family." I led her to confess her anger at God and another sin she felt guilt about and to ask His forgiveness, then I asked the Lord what He wanted her to know. "He's already forgiven me for that" she said. She told me that she no longer felt any anger at God or any feelings of shame or guilt.

With her anger at God out of the way I asked her if she would like to get rid of her grief over the loss of her grandfather and she said that she would. We prayed together and she gave this grief to the Lord and asked Him to carry it for her. I prayed again and asked the Lord if there was anything He wanted her to know and she said, "We'll get to see each other again someday." I asked her how she felt and she said, "My chest isn't so heavy. I still miss him but it's not painful. I feel happy!" she said with a big smile.

Many people are angry at God because of losses or difficult circumstances that He allows them to experience. This leads them to withdraw from Him, quit going to church, and get involved in sinful behaviors in order to feel better. But the Lord is able to take away their anger toward

Him when they are willing to give it to Him. This young woman was willing because she saw how harmful her anger was to her and her children and she was desperate for help. Even good, sincere believers (and preachers) become angry at God, but the solution is simple: be honest with God about your anger toward Him and give it to Him, and He will carry it for you and replace it with His peace.

Summary

When dealing with deaths and losses many people struggle with anger toward God since He is ultimately the one who controls these matters. It is important to know how to help others deal with their anger toward God and not be like Job's friends who tried to give him good advice that was more harmful than helpful. It is wonderful that we don't have to give any advice at all; we can simply lead them to the Lord and let Him speak to them, carry their burdens, and comfort them through His Spirit. He is, after all, the "Wonderful Counselor, Mighty God, Eternal Father, [and] Prince of Peace" (Isaiah 9:6).

Discussion Questions

1. Have you ever become angry at God? If so, what led you to become angry and how did you resolve your anger? Share this with your group.

2. Are you aware now of any anger toward God that you need to release? Would you like to get rid of your anger toward God if you could?

3. Have you ever tried to encourage or help someone who was very angry at God? Were you successful?

4. Do you believe that you would have become angry like Job if you had experienced the serious losses and afflictions that he did?

5. Consider the stories shared in this chapter and list the different ways that anger toward God can affect a person's life.

Personal Application

Try to be very honest and think back to some of the worst times and greatest difficulties that you have ever experienced. Think about your reaction to those difficult times and consider whether you still have some anger toward God for what happened to you. Write out the reasons for your anger toward God, and then pray and ask Him to take your anger from you. Write out any insights that come to your mind and record your feelings afterwards.

CHAPTER 7

Overcoming Guilt
and Shame

asked for a volunteer to pray with at a seminar as a demonstration for the group, and a middle-aged woman volunteered. This was a short seminar and we had only discussed how to overcome feelings of grief and anger. I asked the volunteer what she needed prayer about and she said that her husband had died just nine days earlier. It was still very fresh on her mind, she had listened to me talk about how the Lord can take away our grief and carry it for us, and she really wanted relief from her painful feelings of grief.

When I inquired about her husband she told me that they had been married for fifteen years and they had four children. Her husband unexpectedly died at home from a heart attack. I empathized with her and told her that I was sorry for her loss. Then I asked her what was the main emotion that she felt as she thought about her husband. To my surprise she said that she felt guilt and shame. We had not discussed how to overcome feelings of shame so this group had no idea how to deal with shame.

I asked the woman why she felt shameful and she said that her husband had gone into their bathroom and closed the door, and then collapsed in front of the door, blocking it so that it could not be opened. She tried desperately to open the door to help her husband but was unable to do so. By the time they were able to get inside the bathroom he had died. She felt that it was her fault and believed that if she had tried harder, her husband would still be alive. I prayed for her and asked the Lord, "Lord, is there anything that you want this lady to know about the belief that it is her fault that her husband died and that she should have tried harder?" I told her to be quiet and let me know if she had any thoughts come into her mind.

"It's not my fault," she said. "It was his time to go. There was nothing more that I could do." I asked her if that thought felt true to her and she said that it did. "So, how do you feel now as you think about it being your fault that your husband died? Does that still feel true?" I asked. "No," she said. "I know it wasn't my fault."

"So, what is the main emotion you feel now as you think about the loss of your husband?" I asked her. "I just miss him," she replied. With the feelings of shame gone she was now feeling strong feelings of grief and we were able to focus on those feelings, make a list of everything that she missed about her husband, and give her grief to the Lord. When we were finished she felt peaceful and calm and was no longer feeling any shame, grief, or negative emotions after losing her husband nine days earlier.

I was able to meet with this woman several more times after this to confirm that she was still doing well and experiencing God's peace. The Lord took all her painful emotions and replaced them with His peace so that she could start a new life, be a good mother and provider, and take care of her four children.

Understanding Shame and Guilt

Shame is closely related to guilt. Guilt is a feeling that you have failed and deserve to be punished, based upon factual information. When you know that you have done something that is morally wrong according to God's Word, you should feel some guilt. Whether or not you feel any guilt the fact remains that you are guilty of a moral failure. Someone who commits adultery and is unfaithful to their spouse is morally guilty even if they justify it or experience no feelings of guilt about their behavior. They are factually guilty and may need to learn how to overcome their feelings of guilt once they acknowledge their failure.

Shame, on the other hand, is a feeling that is based upon the belief that you should have done something that you did not do, or a belief that you are dirty, bad, or shameful, or that you deserve to be punished for something that you did or for something that happened to you. People who feel shameful feel guilty, they feel that they are unacceptable, they deserve to be punished, and they are intrinsically dirty and repulsive to others. Shame is an exaggerated sense of guilt, or it can be a completely "false guilt" when the individual condemns themselves for something that happened to them that they could not stop, such as when a child is molested and feels that he is dirty and repulsive because of what an adult did to him.

Whiter than Snow

A man came to me for counseling who had been to prison. He came from a violent home where his father had literally killed his mother and buried her in their back yard, so he had some deep emotional issues in his life. While he was in prison he was saved and became a serious follower of Jesus, and when he was released he regularly got up at 4:30 each morning so he would have time to pray and read his Bible. His wife witnessed this profound change in him and others who knew him liked and respected him because he always had a smile on his face and talked with others about Jesus. I always looked forward to our sessions when we were able to talk about the Lord.

One day when he came to our counseling session he told me, "I need to talk to you about something. When I was a young man I did something that I am very ashamed of, and every time I think about it I feel bad." I asked him if he had talked with the Lord about these things and he said that he had. I asked him if he believed the Lord had forgiven him and he said, "I believe the Lord is a forgiving God and He has forgiven me."

"That's good," I replied, "but do you feel forgiven?"

"No, I don't feel forgiven" he responded.

"Would you like to feel forgiven?" I asked. He said that he would, so I instructed him to close his eyes and think about what he had done that was so shameful, then I prayed and said, "Lord, what do you want this man to know about his belief that he is dirty, bad, and shameful because of these things that he did as a young man?"

This man suddenly burst into tears and began sobbing. I asked him what thought came into his mind and he said, "The thought that popped into my mind when you prayed was 'You're my child.'" I asked him how that made him feel and he said it made him feel good. Then I asked him if I could say another prayer for him and he said I could. I prayed and said, "Lord, is there anything else that you want this man to know about his belief that he is dirty, bad, and shameful because of what he did as a young man?"

He again burst into tears and began sobbing. I asked him what thought had come into his mind this time. "You're already clean, whiter than snow," he said. "Does that feel true to you?" I asked. He said that it did. "How does that make you feel?" I asked. "It makes me feel great!" he said.

"So, think about what you did as a young man that made you feel so shameful," I said. "How do you feel now when you think about that?" "You know" he said, "I know that what I did was wrong, but I also know that I am completely forgiven."

Just like that, this man was set free from his feelings of shame that had held him in bondage for so many years. I have had many opportunities to speak with him since then and he confirms that he still feels free of any feelings of guilt or shame. He knows that the Lord has forgiven him and he feels forgiven.

How to Overcome Genuine Guilt

Genuine guilt is the God-given feeling when we know that we have done something wrong and have violated God's standards. The Bible says, "they show the work of the Law written in their hearts, their conscience bearing witness, and their thoughts alternately accusing or else defending them" (Romans 2:15). We all fail and violate our own consciences at times and the Bible says that "all have sinned and fall short of the glory of God." (Romans 3:23). These feelings of guilt for things we do wrong can deeply affect us in very negative ways. Guilt separates us from God, makes us feel bad about ourselves, and can make us depressed, or lead us to drink or use drugs to feel better.

The man just described felt genuine guilt about something he had done as a young person. He later told me what he had done and it was sinful and harmful to another person. He knew that he had done wrong and he had already confessed it to the Lord and asked His forgiveness.

The only way to deal with genuine guilt is to confess it to God and ask for forgiveness. The Bible says in 1 John 1:9 "If we confess our sins, He is faithful and righteous to forgive us our sins and to cleanse us from all unrighteousness." Sin is a spiritual problem and the only way to remove our guilt is by confessing our failures to God and sincerely asking for His forgiveness through the blood of Jesus.

Mental health professionals have no solution for genuine guilt. I have been in the mental health profession for over thirty-five years now and I have yet to see a workshop or a book written by a mental health professional on the subject of how to overcome guilt. I have seen a few books that devote a few paragraphs or pages to this topic, but they usually tell the reader to simply rationalize, or minimize their guilt and to realize that everyone fails. They may also recommend some medications to numb your feelings, but this will not remove the guilt.

The one exception that I have found to this is when the professionals are dealing with sexual offenders, especially child molesters, and most of them feel that it is therapeutic for the offenders to feel guilty so that they will not reoffend. However, my experience is that such guilt only compounds the problem and makes the offender feel bad and more prone to reoffend. The Scriptures say that the Lord wants to "forgive us our sins and... cleanse us from all unrighteousness." The only solution for genuine guilt is a spiritual solution. Jesus died to pay for all your sins, and when you receive Jesus as your Savior then your sins are forgiven.

Identifying Feelings of Shame

Once you confess your genuine failures and sins, then you can address your feelings of shame as well. If you have already confessed your sins and failures to the Lord and you still feel guilty or shameful, then this is "false guilt" and shame. Shame is based upon our beliefs, and the following are the most common:

- I'm dirty, bad, and shameful because of what I did.
- It was my fault.

- I should have done more.
- I should not have done what I did.
- I should have tried harder or resisted more.
- I'm dirty or disgusting.

Such beliefs are usually deeply rooted in our past memories and experiences and are very difficult to remove. You cannot easily talk people out of these beliefs, and therapists spend years trying to persuade their clients that they are not shameful or responsible for things that happened to them as a child.

Overcoming Feelings of Shame

Although it is difficult to talk people out of these deeply embedded beliefs using traditional mental health techniques, Jesus can remove them very easily. When you know that you have done wrong and you have already confessed it to the Lord and asked His forgiveness, and you still feel shameful and guilty, simply ask the Lord what He wants you to know about your belief that you are shameful. Listen quietly and allow Him to speak to your heart, and He will bring you the truth you need to set you free (John 8:32). If you still feel guilt and shame, then you can take the following three steps:

STEP ONE: Identify the original source of your feelings of shame.
Try to remember the first time you felt this same feeling of guilt and shame, then focus on the memory as the possible source of these feelings. Usually these feelings are rooted in early childhood experience and Satan uses them to keep you in bondage. If you cannot remember any such early experiences, then pray and ask the Lord to take you to the source and origin of your feelings of shame. Quietly focus on your inner

thoughts, and as early memories come to your mind, identify the one that seems to be the earliest.

STEP TWO: Identify the beliefs you have about the event.
The beliefs can be identified by the thoughts that you have about yourself as you think about the event, such as "It is my fault..." or "I am dirty, bad, and shameful because of what happened" or "I should have done_____."

STEP THREE: Pray for truth about the event.
While remembering the event and thinking these thoughts, say a simple prayer and ask the Lord what He wants you to know about those beliefs. Then listen quietly and see what thoughts come into your mind.

When you pray and listen quietly, letting the Lord speak to your heart, He will replace the lies you believe with His truth. When this happens you will be set "free indeed" (John 8:36). If the thoughts that come into your mind when you pray like this come from your own mind, they will not set you free. Isaiah 55:11-12 says,

> So shall My word be which goes forth from My mouth;
> It shall not return to Me empty,
> Without accomplishing what I desire,
> And without succeeding in the matter for which I sent it.
> For you will go out with joy,
> And be led forth with peace.

When God's thoughts come into your mind, they will set you free from bondage and give you peace, just as this Scripture says.

The Damaging Impact of Shame

Shame is a powerful and destructive emotion that Satan uses effectively to destroy lives. Jesus described Satan as "a liar, and the father of lies" (John 8:44) and nowhere is this seen more clearly than in the way he feeds a child with the lie that he is "dirty, shameful, and bad" because of some childhood molestation. Shame is based upon false beliefs or lies that a person believes, and they lead the person to hate themselves, to harm themselves, to think suicidal thoughts, to involvement in unhealthy relationships, and to attempt to punish themselves.

A woman came for help with her nightmares and her fears of her former abusive boyfriend. She had been married for 23 years to her husband who treated her well and never abused her, but she felt neglected so she left him for a younger man. For thirteen years this younger man abused her brutally, beat her, and verbally abused her. He choked her till she almost passed out, strangled her with belts, punched her, kicked her, and tried to run her over with a car. He told her that she was so ugly no man would want her and he told her that her family didn't need her. After abusing her he told her that it was her fault and blamed her for the abuse because of little things she did that upset him. After thirteen years of such abuse he cut himself with a knife and threatened to kill this woman's children and himself if she ever left him. His anger manifested itself outside their home, also, when he almost beat another man to death and was sent to prison for it.

After he had been in prison four years, this woman was still so full of fear, anger and shame that she could not sleep at night because she thought about this man so much and worried about him getting out of prison and hunting her down. She returned to her former husband who lovingly accepted her back, but she was so fearful and traumatized that she was still unhappy. We talked about how to get rid of her anger and made a list of twenty-seven things she resented about her boyfriend. Then I led her in a prayer and she gave the Lord her resentments and asked Him to take them from her, after which I asked the Lord what He wanted her to know. She said, "I will be okay, and I did get away from him." I asked her how that made her feel, and she tearfully said, "That helped me! I don't feel any anger now." "What do you think about that?" I asked her. "He's amazing!" she answered.

I asked her if she had any other negative feelings and she said that she felt guilty and shameful for wasting thirteen years of her life and depriving her family. I prayed for her about these feelings of guilt and shame and asked the Lord what He wanted her to know. She listened quietly to the Lord and said, "My family never stopped loving me" and "I'm doing everything I can to make up for it." I asked her if she had any other negative feelings and she told me that she was no longer fearful because, "I have people who will protect me now." She said she no longer felt any fear, shame, or anger but she felt "Peaceful." She added, "He can't hurt me anymore." I asked her where she got that idea and she pointed up and said, "The Lord."

This woman who entered my office feeling bound up with fear and shame, left with a smile on her face. She said, "I can walk out with a smile on my face. My husband never called me names or mistreated me. Why did I ever leave him? We were together twenty-three years." I explained that when she had been sexually abused as a child, she came to believe that she was dirty, bad, and shameful and she deserved to be punished. Her husband treated her well but she believed the lie from the devil that she needed to be punished, so she left her husband for a young man who abused and punished her. She ended our session by saying, "I prayed previously, but I didn't give my burdens to the Lord until now."

What an amazing example of the power of a lie to destroy a person's life, but it's also an amazing example of the power of truth to set a captive free. She left with a smile on her face, rejoicing in God's amazing grace, and returning home to a good husband who never stopped loving her in spite of her waywardness, just like the Lord who loves his prodigal children and is waiting for them with open arms. At our next session together we talked about her sexual abuse by her stepfather, and as we prayed about it the Lord brought truth to her mind and set her free from the lies that had held her in bondage for so many years.

Man Set Free From Sexual Abuse

I saw a man who wanted help in dealing with some sexual abuse he had experienced as a child. He grew up in a Christian family, but at age seven he was molested by an older cousin one time which made him feel "nasty, disgusted, and shameful" afterwards. Shame is a belief-based emotion that is based upon lies we believe, such as "I am dirty, bad and shameful," so I knew that we needed to pray for truth. He didn't discuss any details, but I prayed for him and asked the Lord what He wanted this man to know about his belief that he was disgusting and shameful. After a period of quiet reflection he said he heard, "I have set you free; you're free because of what I've done." He smiled, relaxed and said he felt no more shame or disgust while thinking about this memory. The Lord brought truth to his mind and set him free of his shame.

This man told me that he began acting out as a teenager, probably as a result of his molestation, and was molested again at age fifteen by a friend while he was high on some drugs. He felt feelings of anger and shame as a result of this incident, so we spoke first about his anger. He was angry at his friend for taking advantage of him when he was high, for violating his trust, and for destroying their friendship. We prayed about these resentments and he asked the Lord to take them from him. After our prayer he said that he felt good and had no more anger toward his former friend, but he still felt some feelings of shame. He said that he believed, "I'm dirty and disgusting because of what this guy did to me." I prayed and asked the Lord what He wanted this man to know. "You are righteous; I made you righteous," were the thoughts that came to his mind, and he told me that he felt "peace" and felt no more anger or shame about this incident. Once again, the truth set him free from feelings of shame over this second incident.

When we were done, this man told me that he felt good and he had no more feelings of anger, guilt, or shame, even while thinking about his sexual abuse. Sexual abuse can have a very negative impact on a child, even when they have a good Christian family. The devil uses such incidents to make them feel dirty and bad even though they did nothing wrong, then he uses this to destroy their lives and lead them into drug abuse, sexual addictions, and anger. It is very difficult to help sexual abuse victims to be set free from the negative impact of their abuse, but the Lord is able to easily set them free from their anger and shame so that the negative impact of the sexual abuse is stopped. Praise God that He is able to set captives free.

No Longer Dirty

A young man came to me who wanted help in dealing with some feelings from being molested as a child. A thirteen-year-old babysitter took advantage of him when he was only seven years old and this left an indelible impression on him. He was full of shame and feelings of helplessness and aloneness, and as a young man he got into fights to prove that he was not weak and helpless. As he grew into manhood he began lifting weights and wearing tattoos to show others that he was not powerless. But his negative feelings led him to abuse drugs and got him into some legal trouble, and he was looking for help.

As he talked about being molested as a child, he hung his head low and avoided eye contact due to his feelings of shame. He said that he felt dirty, shameful, angry and embarrassed about what had happened, and he had never talked about it before. I told him to focus on the memory and his feelings, and then I prayed for him, "Lord, what do you want 'Joe' to know about his belief that he was dirty and shameful because of what happened to him as a child?" I instructed him to let me know if any thoughts came to his mind.

The following thoughts came into his mind. "I was too young to resist him; he was a lot bigger than me. He probably had something similar happen to him. These feelings can be released. It was forced on me but I'm no longer helpless. It wasn't my fault. I'm not alone; I have many people who care for me and who are with me." I asked him if those thoughts felt true to him and he affirmed that they did.

After this I asked him how he felt and he told me that he no longer felt anger or shame. He said he just felt some sadness because the thirteen-year-old boy who had molested him had probably been molested also. The young man smiled and looked relaxed. He was able to talk about the incident and think about it without any embarrassment, shame or anger. The Lord replaced the lies he had been carrying with truth, and this gave him peace.

Afterwards, he talked about how he worked out so hard for so many years to prove that he was not helpless. He told me that he had gotten all of his tattoos as a way of showing others that he was tough and was not helpless, but now he was embarrassed to have them. When he left the session he was a free man, no longer shackled with emotions based upon lies he believed.

Like this young man, Jesus wants each of us to be set free. We do not need to remain in bondage to our past and to our emotions, because

He has come to "set the captives free." Jesus loves you and wants you to know the truth that you are not dirty, helpless, or alone.

Shame and Anger at Oneself

Shame leads to many forms of self-mutilation including cutting oneself, prostituting oneself, body piercings and even tattooing. When working with inmates in prisons and jails the tattoos are obvious and reflect the inner turmoil, anger, and shame of the inmates. I saw a woman in the local jail who had been in and out of jail repeatedly. She said that she was raised by a praying, godly mother and grandmother, and had been a spiritual leader at times to the other women in jail. But she continued to use drugs and to be taken away from her five children whenever she got out.

I had seen this woman in a previous incarceration, but when she returned to jail again this attractive woman had new tattoos on both sides of her face, showing that she was still in bondage to some emotions. As I interviewed her I learned that her mother, grandmother, and sister all had muscular dystrophy, and this woman took care of them and felt much sadness and anger at God for their condition. She began drinking as a teenager, but when her grandmother and sister died she began using drugs heavily and got involved in destructive, abusive relationships with men.

The primary emotion she expressed was anger at herself, which is another name for shame. I asked her why she felt angry at herself and she said it was because of all the things she had done; not taking care of her children, using drugs, and not being around as her children were growing up. I asked her if she had confessed this to the Lord and asked for His forgiveness and she said that she had, and she believed that she was forgiven.

However, when I asked her if she "felt forgiven" she said "no." She said that she didn't feel that she deserved to be forgiven; she deserved to be punished. I prayed for her and asked the Lord what He wanted her to know about that belief. After a minute she opened her eyes and said that she clearly heard the words, "You are forgiven." I asked her if that felt true and she said that it did. I prayed for her again and she said, "I need to move forward. I am a child of His and He loves me." After we finished praying I asked her if she still felt unforgiven and that she deserved to be punished. She smiled and said she felt forgiven and did not deserve to be punished. She looked peaceful and happy, and her feelings of shame were gone.

I identified several losses this woman had and made a prayer plan for a future visit so that she can be set free from all her emotional bondage and end the revolving door. What a joy it is to see men and women like this set free from their emotional bondage so they can live productive lives for the Lord and become good parents and life partners.

Shame from an Abortion

I saw a woman who had had an abortion as a young woman. This woman had a long history of traumas, but the one that she wanted to focus on in our session was a forced abortion that she had had at age seventeen. She stated that she got pregnant at age seventeen and married the baby's father. The young man and his mother, both of whom were church-attending people, put some heavy drugs in her orange juice and drugged her up. They then flew her to another town and kept her drugged while her baby was aborted. She was conscious enough to sign the consent forms, but was so drugged that she didn't really understand what was happening and offered no resistance. Afterwards, she was deeply upset when she learned that her child had been aborted.

She expressed strong feelings of anger, sadness, and guilt when describing this tragic event. We first focused on her anger toward her husband and his mother for drugging her and murdering her child. We made a list of the reasons for her anger, and then we prayed and asked the Lord to take her anger from her. She said that she felt no anger after this. Then we focused on her feelings of sadness at the horrible, painful death the child experienced and its never having a chance to enjoy life. She gave her sadness to the Lord and He took it from her when she gave it to Him in prayer. Finally, we focused on her feelings of shame and guilt. She partially blamed herself for the child's death because she signed the medical forms granting permission for the procedure, she got on the plane, and she did not resist the abortionist. I prayed for her and asked the Lord what He wanted her to know about her feelings of guilt. The thoughts that came to her were, "That baby is in heaven with God" and "It wasn't my fault because I was heavily drugged and forced." I asked her if those thoughts felt true and she affirmed that they did.

After these prayers this woman said that she felt no more sadness, anger, or guilt about this forced abortion. She then felt peaceful and calm while thinking about and talking about her abortion. This event had deeply damaged her emotionally and affected her throughout her entire life, but now she was set free from these painful emotions.

Shame and Marital Problems

A man came for help with marital problems that were rooted in his sexual problems. He had some significant grief and anger issues that needed attention, but he was certain that his problems were rooted in early childhood experiences beginning at age four. When he was four years old a man had exposed himself to him and tried to get him to touch him, but he never did touch him. However, he felt deeply ashamed of what happened and felt he was dirty, so he never told anyone what had happened. The feelings of shame were embedded in his mind at this point and he became fixated on sex at a very early age. At age eleven he had an experience with another child his age and the shame deepened. He felt that this was a turning point for him, that God was done with him, and he was so bad and shameful that even God could not forgive him. With these beliefs firmly embedded in his mind he became entrenched in a pattern of behaviors that lasted for decades.

I asked this man to think about that early childhood experience, remember what had happened, and tell me what he felt and believed. He said that he felt "dirty and ashamed." I prayed and asked the Lord what He wanted this boy (in the memory) to know about those beliefs; I told the man to just be quiet and listen and let me know if any thoughts came to his mind. "I still love you; it wasn't your fault," were the thoughts that came to his mind. I asked him if that felt true and he said that it did. Then I asked him how he felt and he said he felt sad because this childhood event had affected him so profoundly and led to so many wasted years, and he had carried this secret for so long. I led him in a short prayer, telling the Lord why he was sad and asking Him to carry that sadness for him, and then asked the Lord if there was anything He wanted this man to know. "He is still with me; I don't have to carry this any longer; He still loves me," was the response the man received. Then I asked him to think about the childhood event and tell me how he felt. He said he felt "neutral and calm." There were no more feelings of shame or guilt and he did not feel dirty or ashamed anymore.

We talked for a few minutes about some other childhood events and prayed about them. When we were done I prayed for him again and asked the Lord what He wanted this man to know. "You are my child" was the thought that came to his mind. I prayed "Lord, is there anything else?" "I'm not dirty, bad, or disgusting to God," he said. This man smiled and thanked me for spending time with him. He left feeling much lighter and feeling clean and forgiven. That is all it takes to be set free from childhood sexual abuse; just a simple truth from the Lord.

Quick Release of Shame

A man came to a session with me who was very nervous and full of dread. He had received some previous healing but hated to think about being molested by his step-grandfather, and he knew we were going to discuss it. He said that he resented the step-grandfather because he betrayed his trust and that of his mother, he hurt his grandmother through his actions, and his step grandfather made him unable to tell anyone about what happened so he felt very alone. He also said that it ruined his relationship with his grandmother because he tried to stay away from her home after the molesting occurred. Within a few minutes he was crying as he recalled this molestation.

Then I prayed and asked the Lord what He wanted him to know. He said, "I wasn't alone (God was with me); He held me in His arms; I'm safe. It's okay to cry and I didn't do anything wrong." As these thoughts came to his mind from the Lord, this man quit crying and began to calm down. I asked him how he felt and he said, "Not upset; no sadness." I asked him what he thought about this sudden change in feelings and he said, "That's amazing because I thought I did something wrong by going there. I was a little boy and wanted to spend time with my grandmother. There's nothing wrong with that!"

I asked him how he felt while thinking about the molestation. He said, "It's like hearing the story of another person. I feel peaceful!" Twenty minutes after we began he was smiling and peaceful while thinking about the molestation, and yet he had carried this memory for over forty years. Suddenly, he was released from his emotional bondage and shame and could talk about this traumatic event without any negative feelings. How amazing it is that the Lord can set people free so quickly, when they have been in bondage for so many years to such feelings. Jesus sets the captives free from feelings of shame about being molested.

Other Belief-Based Emotions

In Chapter Two we talked about grief as a fact-based emotion, and then we later discussed anger and sadness as fact-based emotions also. The four emotions of grief, anger, sadness, and disappointment are all fact-based emotions, which means that they are not based upon our beliefs but upon factual events that have happened. The reason that we can know they are not based upon false beliefs is because Jesus experienced these four emotions, and He did not have any false beliefs, because He was the Son of God. When we are dealing with fact-based emotions, we cannot talk or reason other people or ourselves out of these feelings. All we can do is be completely honest about them, then give them to the Lord and let Him carry them for us. As we do this, He does take these feelings from us and carries them for us in a miraculous way.

However, there are many other feelings that are based upon false beliefs, lies, or irrational beliefs that we hold. Shame is just one example of a belief-based emotion. In addition to shame, other belief-based emotions are fear, aloneness, helplessness, hopelessness, and worthlessness. Each of these additional emotions can be resolved using the same three steps identified in this chapter for shame. First, identify the source of the emotion, then identify the beliefs connected to the emotion, and last, pray for truth. Whether you are experiencing fear, aloneness, or feelings of worthlessness, this process works effectively to release us from these feelings as we pray and allow the Holy Spirit to replace the lies we believe with His truth.

The Lord is truly the "Wonderful Counselor" of Isaiah 9:6, and Jesus promised that when He left He would send us the Holy Spirit, who He said would "guide you into all the truth" (John 16:13). It is a wonderful thing to witness the Lord setting men and women free from shame, fear, and other emotions that keep us in bondage. The Lord does not want us to be stuck in these feelings, because they weigh us down and prevent us from being able to serve Him freely. The prophet Isaiah recorded the words of the Lord in Isaiah 1:18,

> Come now, and let us reason together,
> Says the LORD,
> Though your sins are as scarlet,
> They will be as white as snow;
> Though they are red like crimson,
> They will be like wool.

Discussion Questions

1. Do you know anyone who engages in irrational behaviors that repeatedly lead them to get involved in destructive relationships? Can you see how they have shame that leads them into this pattern of behavior?

2. Have you ever felt angry at yourself for something that happened or something you did in the past, that you have confessed to God, about which you still feel guilty?

3. If you could get rid of those feelings of guilt and shame, would you like to?

Personal Application

Try to be very honest and think back to things you have done in the past about which you still feel guilty. If you have never explicitly talked with the Lord about this, and confessed your sin and failure and asked for His forgiveness, do that now. Then, think about what you have done and see if you feel completely forgiven or if you still feel guilty. If you still feel guilty about something after confessing it, pray and ask the Lord what He wants you to know about it. Write down the thoughts that come to your mind and write down your new feelings afterwards. Continue to pray and ask for truth until you are completely free from feelings of guilt and shame.

If you have multiple experiences from the past that make you feel shameful, such as sexual abuse, pray about each one of these memories. Focus on one at a time, recall what happened and what makes you feel shameful. Specifically identify the belief you had such as: "It was my fault," or "I should have done something different" or "I am dirty, bad, or shameful because of what happened." Then, pray for truth and ask the Lord what He wants you to know about the memory. Write down the thoughts that come to your mind. If they are from the Lord, it will set you free from your feelings of shame so that you can remember the event without any negative feelings connected to it. Share your experience with the group or ask for help from someone in the group if you do not get complete healing.

CHAPTER 8

Overcoming Relationship Losses

osses can come in many forms besides deaths, and all types of losses can be painful. Many people report that the divorce of their parents was not only painful, but had a long-lasting, negative impact on their life. Those who experience a divorce often report that their divorce was more painful than any other loss in their lives, because their loss was not due to an accident or unavoidable death but to a choice by their partner to permanently sever a relationship that they thought would last for a lifetime. Even romantic breakups can be very devastating and impact an individual for a long time, sometimes leading to suicide. Whatever the form of the loss, it can cause severe emotional pain and lead to the negative consequences of depression, addiction, anger, violence, relationship problems, and spiritual problems.

Many studies have shown a relationship between parental loss and depression. The "Virginia Twin Study," mentioned in Chapter One, was conducted by researchers Kenneth S. Kendler and Carol A. Prescott, to understand the causes of psychiatric and substance abuse disorders. In their book *Genes, Environment, and Psychopathology* (Kendle and Prescott, 2006) they document their findings with regard to the impact of parental deaths and divorces on the development of mental disorders. They found a specific association between parental deaths in childhood and depression, but they found a stronger and more general association between parental divorce and a wide variety of mood, anxiety, and substance abuse disorders. In addition, they found that the risk of psychological problems associated with parental divorce lasted much longer than those for parental death, especially for substance abuse disorders and alcohol abuse, which never decreased over the years. In simple lay terms this means that divorce has a much more damaging psychological impact upon a child than parental death. Parental death is related to the development of depression, but parental divorce is strongly related to the development of a wide range of psychological problems that may last throughout the individual's lifetime.

Set Free from Painful Divorce

I was invited to a Christian recovery meeting and asked to share about Set Free Prayer Ministry. I explained how the Lord had taught me how he can set people free from addictions as they release their feelings of grief, anger, and shame through prayer. The group was very attentive, and when I asked for a volunteer, a man threw his hand up immediately and volunteered. He said that he would like some prayer about his divorce. He stated that he had been married fourteen years, and then three years ago his wife divorced him and took their three children with her, after which he began using drugs heavily. He broke down and began sobbing in front of the group; he was obviously very emotionally torn about this divorce.

I asked the man what emotions he felt as he thought about his divorce and he said that he felt guilt and grief. He felt very guilty and shameful for not visiting his children, because it was so painful for him to see them and not be able to live with them and raise them. He denied initially that he was angry and said that he had already forgiven his ex-wife, but as he talked it was apparent that he still had some anger. I suggested to him that we start with his anger, because anger prevents us from hearing from the Lord, and he agreed. I asked him what made him angry at his wife, and he told me that she cheated on him, she lied about the other man and said that he was a homosexual, and then she left him for this other man. It also made him angry that she took their children from him, and coached them to lie to him about the other man, and then she took everything from him in the divorce.

I led him in a prayer and he told the Lord these six resentments he had, and he asked the Lord to take away his anger from him. Then I prayed and asked the Lord if there was anything that He wanted this man to know. "He wants me to forgive her; the babies need us to get along," he said. "He forgives me for overlooking them and not paying attention to them, and for using drugs. They miss me and love me," he added. His mood suddenly changed and he quit crying and began smiling as he talked. I asked him how he felt now as he thought about his divorce and he said, "I love her; she's a good mother to them." He said that he had no more anger.

The entire group was amazed at his dramatic change of mood and attitude. He felt no more anger or shame from his divorce, but he still felt sad and missed his children, so I asked him what he missed about them. He told me that he missed their smiles and laughter, watching them play, looking into their eyes and telling them that he loved them, being with them, and hearing their childish noises. He talked about the youngest child and her sweetness, and he said that he missed his children's love and affection, having them crawl in bed with him, and just watching them grow up each day. We made a list of twelve things he missed about his children. Then I led him in another prayer and he gave his grief and sadness to the Lord. I asked the Lord again what He wanted this man to know and he said, "He wants me to know they are ok and they miss me and love me. He wants me to do well." After this I asked him how he felt as he thought about his children and he said, "I love them. I feel peace. I feel great!"

This man who was so distraught over his divorce and the loss of his wife and children was transformed from brokenness and bitterness to peace and joy in just a few minutes. The Lord heard his cry and took his burden of anger and grief from him and replaced it with His perfect peace and joy. What a joy it is to see the Lord setting captives free!

The Emotional Impact of Divorce

Divorce can be a devastating experience, both for the divorcing parents and for the children. For the partners it can be devastating, lead to long-term depression, damage their relationships with others (including their children), lead to substance abuse, interfere with their job performance, and lead to impulsive decisions about new relationships. One woman had been depressed for twenty-five years and had begun abusing alcohol because of her divorce. After a couple of sessions in which she released her anger and grief she was suddenly free of her emotional bondage to her former husband and she was able to see him and speak with him without any difficulty. She was also able to remain sober after that, and began rebuilding her life and planning for her future.

Divorce can also have a profound and long-term impact on the children of the divorcing parents. It can lead to anxiety disorders, depression, angry outbursts, oppositional behavior, and substance abuse. The impact of the divorce on the child can last their entire life. However, the good news is that it is possible to release all the negative feelings resulting from a divorce so that you do not carry them with you and allow them to damage your life. The Lord wants you to release these emotions and allow Him to carry them for you.

In order to remove the negative emotional impact of a divorce it is necessary to identify the individual emotions you are experiencing and to deal with each of them. Fortunately, these emotions usually fall into the following four categories: grief, anger, sadness, and shame. It is important to recognize the emotions you are experiencing and then to deal separately with each of them.

Anger is frequently experienced by those affected by divorce. For the involved adults it may be anger about many incidents from their past, it may be anger about an affair, anger about the legal or financial matters relating to the divorce, or numerous other matters. Children affected by divorce may be angry at one or both parents due to their perception of who caused the divorce and how it affected their lives.

Loss of a spouse through divorce, or loss of a family unit for a child, usually triggers off strong feelings of grief that need to be dealt with separately from anger, both by the spouses and the children. This grief is not based upon distorted thinking, but it needs to be acknowledged and released through the prayer-based process described previously. The longer one holds onto this grief, the greater the likelihood that it will lead to negative consequences in the individual's life.

Sadness is a separate emotion that often affects those who have experienced a divorce. There are some aspects of a divorce that are definitely sad and need to be identified and released. For example, it is sad that the family unit has been destroyed, it is sad that the children cannot live with both parents, it is sad that one spouse may be unable to witness the daily life and development of their children, and it is sad that divorce often damages other relationships, such as relationships with church friends and grandparents. Once you recognize these feelings of sadness, you should take yourself or others through the simple steps given in Chapter Four.

Guilt and shame are also very common in divorcing couples who recognize that they may have contributed to the marital break-up, and many times they blame themselves for aspects of the divorce over which they had no control. For example, an affair can occur due to no failure on the part of the abandoned spouse, but this spouse can blame himself or herself for it. Children often blame themselves, erroneously, for their parents' divorce, and this is false guilt or shame. Such feelings of guilt and shame need to be addressed and resolved, or they can lead to long-term damage in the person's life.

Full recovery from divorce occurs when an individual identifies the various emotions they are experiencing and resolves each of them, one by one. The end result will be that they will experience God's peace again, so that talking about or thinking about the divorce or the former partner does not provoke feelings of grief, anger, sadness or shame. Even though things may change drastically after a divorce, the Lord wants to give you His peace and comfort as you learn to cast all your cares upon Him and to replace the lies you believe with His truth. He loves you still and wants you to experience full recovery, so that you will continue to grow in your faith and follow Him.

Set Free from Anger toward Former Husband

A woman came to a Set Free meeting and asked for prayer about her anger toward her ex-husband. She said that her friends and family used to compliment her on her "warm and fuzzy voice," but she had become bitter and angry after her divorce fifteen years earlier. While married, her husband was emotionally abusive and used the Bible as a weapon, by telling her to be submissive to him; then he had multiple affairs.   After their divorce he spitefully told her that he never loved her or wanted to marry her. He was irresponsible and never provided financial support for her and their children, so she had to raise the children alone for many years, which was a severe burden and stress. He treated their daughter terribly because she looked so much like her. He even challenged her faith when he was with her, but he spoiled their son and treated him like a king so that he became very egotistical. In spite of his financial neglect and emotional abuse of his children, he acted like a doting father in public so everyone would think he was a good father. Fifteen years of this treatment had made this woman resentful instead of warm and cheerful as she had previously been.

I asked her if she would like to get rid of this anger and she said that she would. I explained that the first step was just to be honest and to identify all her resentments toward her husband, which we had just done. The second step was to tell the Lord her resentments and ask Him to take them from her, and she was willing to do this. So, I led her in a prayer as she the Lord why she was so angry at her former husband, and then she asked the Lord to take her anger from her and carry it for her. Afterwards, I asked her how she felt and she said, "I'm free of this. I'm at peace." I asked her if she felt any anger, and she said that she had no more anger, but she had some sadness that her ex-husband was missing out on some amazing kids, that her kids don't get to see their little sister, and that they have started becoming angry. We prayed about this sadness and she gave it to the Lord. After that she said that she felt, "neutral, calm, and relaxed."

Since then she has repeatedly affirmed that she is still peaceful and calm about her ex-husband and has no more anger toward him, and her "warm and fuzzy" voice has come back. She was set free from fifteen years of anger in a single prayer session.

Set Free from Anger at Parents' Divorce

There are many children who are angry toward a parent and have become angry or depressed because of their parents' divorce. It often leads to rebelliousness, depression, suicidal thoughts, or drug abuse, but Jesus is able to take these feelings and set them free. I saw a young man who was very depressed and was having suicidal thoughts. Knowing that most depression is rooted in loss, I asked him when his depression began. He told me that it began after his father divorced his mother and left the family. The young man lost his grandfather at age ten, and when his father divorced his mother and left her two years later, he became very depressed and angry. I prayed with him first about the loss of his grandfather. We made a list of twelve things he missed about his grandfather and then gave it to the Lord in prayer, asking the Lord to take it from him and carry it for him. After praying, the young man said he felt no more sadness and felt "kind of happy." This is the first time he had ever prayed for God to take some feelings from him and carry them, and he was pleasantly surprised to see how well it worked.

Then we talked about the loss of his father and his anger toward his father for leaving the family. He was angry that his father left them, quit talking with his children, hurt their mother, screamed at her, and then remarried and started a new family without any regard for his first family. We made a list of nine reasons for the young man's anger. He prayed and gave his anger to the Lord and asked Him to take it from him. After the prayer he said he still felt angry, so I asked him why he was still angry, and he said that his father left them and didn't try to be a father. We prayed about this and gave it to the Lord, but he said that he still felt angry. I've learned that when prayer does not give complete peace it usually means that we missed something, so I asked him again why he was still angry. He told me that he couldn't believe that any parent would do that to a child, his brother was deeply hurt by his father's abandonment and began using drugs, his sisters were so hurt that they became depressed, and he had become depressed also by his father's selfish actions. We then prayed a third time and gave these resentments to the Lord and asked Him to take them from him.

After this third prayer I asked the Lord if there was anything that He wanted this young man to know. "Everyone is okay now," he said. I asked him how he felt now and he said, "I don't feel angry. It helped us to learn not to grow up and make the same mistake with our children." He was surprised, again, to see how the Lord took his anger from him and gave him peace about his father. I asked him what emotion he felt and he said, "Calm." All of his anger had left him and he felt peaceful and calm while thinking about his father.

Resolving Anger toward Former Wife

I saw a man whose wife left him unexpectedly after thirteen years of marriage and took their daughter from him. He had always tried his hardest to be a good husband and father, and it broke his heart when she left him with no explanation and tried to keep him from seeing his daughter. He had to pay over $700 per month for child support even when he lost his job due to health problems. In addition to the anger and grief that he felt from this divorce, it was more painful to him that she received primary custody of their daughter, giving him so little control over her life. His ex-wife was a poor example to her daughter, allowing boyfriends to stay overnight with her and drinking in front of her. When his daughter received some inappropriate texts from a boy, this man had little power to intervene due to her mother's lack of concern. It was upsetting to him that she always had the last say about their daughter.

As we discussed these concerns it became clear that he had a lot of justified anger toward his wife. I asked him if he would like to get rid of those resentments if he could, and he said that he would. We made a list of his resentments toward his ex-wife. He said he resented her manipulations and control; her leaving him when he was giving one-hundred per-cent effort in their marriage; her taking their daughter from him and trying to keep him from seeing her; her laziness and making him do the cooking, cleaning, and laundry when they were married; and her show of favoritism to her other two children. We made a list of eighteen resentments, and then I asked him if he would be willing to tell God these resentments and ask Him to take them from him. He was willing, so we prayed and named each resentment and asked the Lord to take them from him. Then, I asked the Lord if there was anything that He wanted this man to know.

"I remember asking God to be there when I couldn't. I have to trust God to be there. God has the last say," he said. "How does that make you feel?" I asked. "No anger. God will take care of it; God won't fail me." I asked him again how he felt and he said, "Peace. I can trust Him and He has already begun to restore my relationship with my children since I've begun releasing my anger and resentments."

Divorce can be very traumatic, even worse than a loss by death because it is intentional, but the Lord heals the brokenhearted and sets the captives free. Imagine what would happen if every divorced person found this kind of healing from the Lord and turned back to Him, and the church got the reputation as a place where people can find healing and restoration like this. Imagine what would happen if every man was to release his resentments, like this man, and pray for his children and allow the Lord to begin to restore his relationships with his children.

Dealing with Grief over Divorce from Wife

At one of my seminars I asked for a volunteer who had some unresolved grief who would like to experience emotional healing. A man spoke with me during a break and told me that he had been through a divorce a year ago from his wife of twenty years. He wasn't sure if he had any unresolved issues, but as we spoke it sounded like there was some grief over the loss of his wife, and I asked him if he would be willing to pray in front of the group. He said that he was willing to do this, but he was really unsure whether he had anything to pray about.

After the break we gathered together again, and I invited him to come to the front and gave him a microphone. I asked him what he missed about his wife, and as he began talking he immediately burst into tears, saying how he missed calling her his "China doll." It was obvious that he deeply loved her and missed her, even though he thought he had no unresolved feelings. He slowly began to recall everything that he enjoyed about her such as her beautiful blonde hair, her eyes, her tiny fingers and feet, and her perfume. He talked about her personality characteristics that he missed such as her love for people, the way she loved their children, her cheerfulness, and her encouragement to him spiritually. He said he missed going to church with her, the awesome meals she fixed after church, the ministry they did together, and just sitting with her on the couch and combing her hair. He cried through each of these memories and the audience wept with him, until we had a list of twenty-nine things he missed about his wife.

I then led him in a prayer as he cried through each item he named, and then he gave his sadness and grief to the Lord. I prayed and asked the Lord what He wanted this man to know. "It will be okay," he said. I asked him how he felt and he said he felt peaceful and a lot lighter. I probed to see if there was any more grief or sadness and he said there was none; he just felt peaceful and calm. The man's pastor was present, and he tearfully asked forgiveness for not helping him with his grief. This brought more tears to the eyes of many people. Everyone was "amazed at the greatness of God" (Luke 9:43).

Dealing with Shame

Many people who go through a divorce experience feelings of guilt and shame after their divorce. Sometimes their guilt is genuine because they have contributed significantly to the conflicts in the marriage. In such cases I ask them to list the ways in which they failed in their marriage, and to confess them to the Lord and ask for His forgiveness. Then, if they still feel shameful, I pray for them and ask the Lord what He wants them to know. In other cases, a spouse may experience false guilt, or shame, about their failures.

Women often blame themselves for their husband's infidelity or pornography addiction because they are not as sexually attentive to their husband as he wished. One woman sought counseling after her husband admitted to being addicted to pornography and having relationships with prostitutes. She felt that it was her fault that she was not more attentive to him physically and she did not try harder to make herself attractive to him. I prayed and asked the Lord what He wanted her to know about her belief that it was her fault that her husband turned to prostitutes and pornography because she did not make herself more attractive. The Lord brought truth to her mind and told her that it had nothing to do with her appearance, but that her husband had a problem. Her feelings of false guilt and shame were suddenly resolved, and we then focused on her feelings of anger and grief over the loss of her marriage.

Romantic Breakups

Men and women often struggle with painful emotions after a romantic relationship ends. A woman came for help with her anxiety and grief after her boyfriend left her. She began having anxiety attacks and nightmares, and she was sleeping only two hours per night. She was skeptical that prayer would work, but we made a list of the things that she missed about her ex-boyfriend and she asked the Lord to take her grief from her. When she left the first session she said she felt no grief or sadness and she felt lighter, and she said with a big smile, "I feel a lot better than I have in a long time!"

When she returned the following week she said that she hadn't cried all week, she had had no more nightmares, and she had slept at least five hours each night. She said, "That's just miraculous! I was really shocked." She also stated that she was able to talk to her former boyfriend without feeling any hate or anger, even though he talked with her about his new girlfriend. However, she admitted that she resented him talking about his girlfriend with her, so we made a list of three other resentments she had, she prayed, and she gave them to the Lord, after which she felt no resentments toward him. She admitted that she had provoked her boyfriend in a number of ways, so she asked the Lord to forgive her. Then I prayed and asked the Lord what He wanted her to know or do and she listened quietly and said, "I need to forgive myself and ask my ex to forgive me."

After this second session she said that she felt no more anger, grief, or guilt about her ex. She was set free from all of these emotions so that she could feel God's peace and be a better mother to her children. All her nightmares, anxiety attacks, sleeplessness, anger, and resentment were removed by the Lord as she learned to cast all her anxieties and cares upon Him. She was initially very skeptical that the Lord could help her through prayer, but then after praying she was amazed and shocked at how quickly she was set free from her emotional struggles.

Obsessive Relationships

I met a Christian woman who was carrying strong feelings of guilt and shame about her emotional involvement with a married man. Both she and the gentleman were strong Christians who were knowledgeable about the Bible and were leaders in their churches. She consulted with him about some family issues and he gave her some helpful advice and showed her some kindness. They had been friends for years and their friendship had always been wholesome and appropriate, until one day she started to fall and he caught her. While holding her he kissed her and she felt an overpowering rush of feelings for him. She had never been involved with another man or desired it, but the affection he gave her was overwhelming because she was so lonely since her husband never showed her any affection, held her hand, or said kind things to her. He was an honest and good Christian man, but was emotionally cold to her and never even hugged her, leaving her to cry herself to sleep many nights out of loneliness. This other man was also lonely and felt unfulfilled in his marriage, because his wife was emotionally cold to him and he had never experienced physical pleasure in their marriage.

After the kiss, they began to meet together secretly to talk and go for walks. Although they never engaged in any sexual contact, she enjoyed sitting with him with his arm around her while he said sweet things to her. They both knew it was wrong, but the excitement they felt was so strong that it was overpowering their consciences. She said that she had always been lonely and had never experienced such strong feelings or felt this kind of "young love." It made her feel wonderfully loved for the first time in her life. For months they continued this secret relationship, and both of them felt guilty and shameful. Her prayer life was destroyed, and she couldn't lead Bible studies anymore because she felt like such a hypocrite.

Both of them were so overwhelmed with guilt that they decided they had to end the relationship. Although she knew it was the right thing to do, she could not quit thinking about him and longing to see him and talk with him. She prayed desperately and begged the Lord to take him out of her mind and life, but every time she tried to pray he jumped into her mind. I explained to this woman that she was experiencing grief over the loss of her relationship and that she needed to do two things: First, she needed to be honest and identify what she missed about this gentleman and then secondly, she needed to tell the Lord what she missed about him and ask Him to take her grief and sadness from her. So she began her list. She said she missed his love and affection, his kind words, his hugs and comfort, him sitting with his arm around her, and their intimate conversations each week. She also missed his occasional phone calls, hearing him call her sweet names, and the feeling of "fire" of being in love for the first time.

After making this list she sincerely prayed for the Lord to take her grief and sadness away. I asked her how she felt and she said she still longed to see him and wanted him out of her heart but not out of her life. She still felt some longing for him so I knew we had missed some of the losses. She said she also missed spending time with him, going for walks with him at night, and going to his house when his wife was gone. We prayed again and she gave these additional losses to the Lord. When I asked her how she felt she said she now felt sad, because she met him so late in life, and this intimate relationship had happened innocently without any intention. She also was sad to know that there was no future with him and they had to ignore each other when around mutual friends to avoid any suspicion of their feelings for one another. She said she wanted to be able to witness again and to have a clean heart. We prayed about these feelings of sadness and gave them to the Lord, just as I would with any other loss, and then I asked the Lord what He wanted her to know.

"Peace will come; I was disobedient so God wouldn't hear me, but we have an advocate with the Father." These thoughts felt true to her because they were whispered to her by the Lord, but then she said, "You reap what you sow and you deserve to be miserable." I knew that this thought was not from the Lord, so I prayed and asked the Lord if that was true, and asked what He wanted her to know about that thought. She then said, "God is a loving God; He forgives me. I know I'm forgiven; He doesn't want me to be miserable. He is a loving God. He wants me to rejoice and be glad. He loves me even though I failed." She told me that these thoughts felt true, and they were.

I asked her to think about her gentleman friend again and tell me how she felt. This time she said that she felt better and she felt some hope. Then she said, "The Lord has a plan for my life." Now she could think about this man without the painful longing for him that she had felt before, and she said she felt "good, peaceful, and restful." The next day she told me with excitement that she was free! She still felt peaceful, and calm, and free of the deep longing she had before and the constant, painful obsession with this man. She was no longer thinking about him or wishing to see him again. She thanked me for my help, and praised God for His goodness, love, and power. A month later she affirmed to me that she was still doing well and remained free of her obsession with this man.

Relationships can be very addictive and powerful, even without sexual involvement, and can be very difficult to break. But Jesus heals the brokenhearted, including those who become emotionally trapped in an unholy relationship and are unable to break those bonds. He is able to heal our broken hearts and to fill us with His love, joy, and peace when we learn to be completely honest with Him and give our burdens to him in prayer. What a mighty God we have who is worthy of our praise!

I often encounter Christians who have gotten into a relationship that they know is wrong but which they do not have the strength to end. A Christian woman broke into tears as she told me about a relationship she had with a man whom she had known from childhood. This man was her closest friend, was very loving to her and made her feel special, but he used drugs and she knew that she could never have a godly relationship with him. Over the years they had spent time together, had long telephone conversations, and shared their dreams and feelings together. But as he grew older his addiction increased, and she felt a great loss as he became increasingly impaired. She knew that she needed to end their relationship, but she felt such a strong attachment to him that she could not. She had tried to pray on her own but was not able to get rid of these strong feelings.

I asked her if she would like to get rid of these feelings of grief and sadness and she said that she would. I explained that she first needed to be completely honest about what she missed about him. We identified nineteen things she missed about him. Then I told her that the second thing she needed to do was to pray and tell the Lord what she missed about her friend, and ask Him to take her grief from her.

She prayed and asked the Lord to take her grief from her. After this prayer she said that she felt better and she felt less intense feelings of grief, but she still felt some sadness. We talked about the reasons for her sadness and she said that she was sad because of how he had wasted his life, how he continued to abuse drugs, how unhappy he was, and how they could never have a godly relationship together in spite of their closeness. Through many tears and using many tissues she told the Lord seven reasons for her sadness, and then asked Him to take her sadness from her and carry it for her. After this second prayer she quit crying and said that she felt much better. She was able to smile and not feel the intense sadness and grief about her friend that she had felt previously.

From many similar experiences I have learned that such destructive emotional bonds as these can be broken to free people from their intense sadness and grief so that they are no longer stuck in a compulsive, sinful relationship. Romantic relationships can be very intense and obsessive, but the Lord can heal these in the same way as with other relationship losses. Whether the loss is a friendship that ends after a move, children who move away from home and become distant, a pastor who leaves to pastor another church, or any other loss, the Lord wants to carry that sadness and grief for us and give us His peace.

Discussion Questions

1. When you think about past relationships, what feelings did you have when the relationship ended? How long did it take you to get completely over the loss?

2. Have you had any close friends, pastors, or relatives move away or break off your relationship? How did that feel, and how long did it take you to get over the loss?

3. Do you still have some unresolved feelings from a past relationship that you would like to release today?

Personal Application

Think back to past relationships that you have lost. Do you have any negative feelings about anyone that you have known in the past, with whom you had been very close but who abruptly ended their relationship with you? Try to identify what feelings you still have that are unresolved. Do you have any feelings of grief, anger, or shame about these past relationships? If you still feel badly about a relationship, pray about each emotion and try to resolve them. Share your experience with your class members and ask one of them to pray with you if you cannot completely resolve your negative feelings.

CHAPTER 9

Dealing with Suicides

When I was a child I attended a small, evangelical church that provided me a good doctrinal foundation and taught me that the Bible had the answers to our life problems. My parents were both Christians and my father was a very strong believer who loved to read the Bible and share the gospel with others. He had been radically changed through his conversion, and he taught us good character and moral principles. He also taught me to memorize Scriptures, including 2 Corinthians 5:17, "If any man is in Christ, *he is* a new creature; the old things passed away; behold, new things have come."

At eight years of age I received the Lord as my Savior and began my journey in the Christian life. During the next ten years of life I continued to attend this church. I began to observe my fellow-believers and learned that many of them had serious emotional problems. As a very young boy I attended the wedding of a young couple and then, to my shock, a few years later that young lady committed suicide. It was never discussed publicly, but it had a profound impact upon my life. I learned that many sincere Christians struggle with depression, and they sometimes commit suicide. What I was to learn later was that my experience in this small church was typical of what Christians are like in churches all across the country.

Fifty years later I was a member of another church in which the church secretary committed suicide and shocked the entire church. No one knew or even suspected that she was depressed. She was frequently seen on stage operating the overhead projector and computer system, or helping hand out awards to children in the Awana club. Her husband was a leader in the church and she had frequent contact with the other church leaders. One day she suddenly rushed out of the church building, drove to the schools to speak to her children for the last time, then went to a prominent location in town and shot herself. Such events have a dramatic impact on those around them and close to the suicide victims. Suicide can affect people in many ways, including increasing the likelihood that other family members will commit suicide in the future.

Youth Leader Set Free from Suicide Trauma

I conducted a seminar in 2012 and provided some training to a large group of youth ministers. After the first hour in which I gave an overview of the ministry principles, I asked for a volunteer who would like to resolve some feelings of grief. A young woman came forward for prayer. She said that her brother had committed suicide three years before and she was the last one he called before taking his life. As she spoke, the tears began to flow and the audience became silent and attentive. I explained that when there is a suicide the surviving friends and family members often have mixed feelings of grief, sadness, anger, and shame, and I asked what emotions she felt. She stated that she felt sadness and missed her brother.

I asked the young woman what she missed about him and she began tearfully talking about how she missed his presence, watching him
play with her children and being a good uncle to them, hearing his jokes
and laughter, witnessing his friendliness to people, and seeing his big,
brown eyes. She also missed hanging out with him, talking with him, and
mothering him since he was much younger than she was. After completing the list of losses I led her in a prayer as she told the Lord what she
missed about her brother and asked Him to carry her pain for her. Then
I asked the Lord if there was anything that He wanted her to know. She
said, "It's okay." She said she felt "calm and blank."

She still looked a little tearful so I asked if she felt some sadness
and she said that she did. She was sad because she was helpless to do
anything to prevent his suicide, he was too young to die, her children
lost their uncle, he wouldn't get to see her kids grow up, and she would
never see him get married and have a family. We prayed about these
feelings of sadness and she gave them to the Lord; then I asked the Lord
again if there was anything that He wanted her to know. "There's nothing I could have done" was the response she received. She hadn't stated
that she felt any feelings of shame or that she should have been able
to do something, but she apparently felt this way, and these thoughts
she received from the Lord removed that feeling. Now she said she felt
"peace and calm." I asked if there were any other negative feelings and
she admitted that she felt some anger at her parents and other brother
because her father was not a good father, her mother did nothing when
warned about her son's mental state, and her other brother was such
a poor role model and did nothing to help his brother when he asked
for help. We prayed and she gave her anger to the Lord and asked Him
to carry it for her. After this prayer she said that her anger was gone
now and she felt complete peace and calm. Later that day, she told
the church youth minister that she and her husband had driven to her

brother's grave site. The youth minister asked her how the visit went; all that she said was, "God is amazing! Thank you!"

Suicides can be devastating to the family and friends of the deceased and lead to depression, anger, and substance abuse. The Lord set this young woman free from her feelings of grief, sadness, shame and anger that resulted from her brother's suicide, and now she can pray with her children and family to see them set free from this pain also. We had an incredible time and everyone left encouraged and excited about Jesus.

The Emotional Impact of Suicides

The example given above illustrates the various ways in which suicides typically affect others emotionally. Grief, of course, is likely to be present when someone commits suicide and their friends and family members lose a close friend or relative. They need help in articulating the various memories and characteristics that they miss about the person. Anger is very commonly connected to losses by suicide because the act creates such emotional devastation that it is very hurtful to others close to them. Sadness is also very common. It is sad to know that someone is so unhappy and desperate that they will go to such extreme measures as ending their life. People may need assistance in identifying the reasons for their sadness so that they can give them to the Lord and not continue to carry them indefinitely. Finally, guilt and shame are very often present as close friends and family members blame themselves for not being able to help the person, or for not even knowing that they were depressed.

Pastor's Son Commits Suicide

On April 5, 2013 Pastor Rick Warren of Saddleback Church and author of *The Purpose-Driven Life* was shocked by the suicide of his youngest son.

His 27-year-old son, Matthew, tragically took his own life with an unregistered gun he purchased over the internet. Standing before his church Warren said, "he suffered from mental illness resulting in deep depression and suicidal thoughts" and he went on to say, "In spite of America's best doctors, meds, counselors, and prayers for healing, the torture of mental illness never subsided" (Alvear, Diana 2013). The suicide death of Warren's son sent a shock wave across their 20,000- member church and across the nation.

It was almost four months later before Pastor Warren returned to his church's pulpit. On July 27, 2013, he spoke to his church at a nationally televised service saying, "For twenty-seven years, I prayed every day of my life for God to heal my son's mental illness. It was the number one prayer of my life. It just didn't make any sense why this prayer was not being answered." He also stated that he was in shock for at least a month, and that this tragic event had motivated him to devote himself to the task of addressing the need of the church to help those suffering from mental illness, and to remove the stigma of mental illness. He said that those who suffer from a mental illness and have "a broken brain should be no more ashamed of it than those who have a broken leg." The next six Sundays he preached a sermon series entitled, "How to get through what you're going through." He devoted a message to each of the "Six states of grief: Shock, sorrow, struggle, surrender, sanctification, and service."

In his first public interview after the suicide death of his son, on September 18, 2013 Warren remarked, "I have cried every single day since Matthew died." His wife, Kay Warren, was shocked and offended by friends who implied that a year later she should have moved on. In April 2014, Kay wrote on her Facebook saying, "I am shocked by some subtle and not-so-subtle comments indicating that perhaps I should be ready to move on." She was hurt by those who insinuated that the

Warrens should have already resolved their grief and loss, and went on to say that the old Rick and Kay were gone and "we will never be the same."

Keeping his word to address this important issue, on March 28, 2014 Warren convened one of the largest ever one-day gatherings of Christian leaders focused on the role of churches in addressing mental illness. Teaming up with Bishop Kevin Vann of the Roman Catholic Diocese of Range, and the National Alliance on Mental Illness, they organized "The Gathering on Mental Health and the Church" to lead churches and spiritual leaders across the country to begin talking about mental illness and providing ministry to those suffering (Flacus, 2014).

Man's Solution to Suicidal Depression

Pastor Warren's comment that individuals who suffer from depression have a "broken brain" suggests that he is leading Christians to embrace the view introduced and promoted by pharmaceutical companies, that mental illnesses are the result of chemical imbalances and a broken brain, and the only solution is to take pills. This is not surprising, because our churches are full of physicians and educated people who have been schooled in the same universities and taught this same philosophy. In a $20-million study of U.S. adults called "The National Co-morbidity Study," it was estimated that 48% of all Americans will experience some form of mental illness in their lifetime, and three-fourths of them will do so by age twenty-four, using their broad definition of "mental disorders" (Cromie, William J. 2005). The solution recommended for these disorders is early screening and "treatment" (medication). The director of the study, Thomas Insel, M.D., was disappointed to learn from the study that about a third of people rely solely on nonprofessional sources and spiritual advisors. He commented, "You wouldn't rely on your priest for treatment if you had breast cancer. Why would you go to your priest for a major depressive disorder? These are real medical and brain disorders, and they need to be treated that way" (Cromie, 2015).

In contrast, Harvard-trained psychiatrist Peter Breggin, M.D., has been studying this issue and writing for over four decades about the dangerous side-effects of psychiatric medications, and attempting to counter this doctrine. In his 2008 books, *Medication Madness* and *Brain-Disabling Treatments in Psychiatry*, Dr. Breggin presents compelling evidence that many psychiatric medications cause brain injury, depression, suicidality, hallucinations, delusions, panic attacks, and severe mania, and that antidepressants not only do not work any better than placebos, but often cause depression and other serious problems. He stated that in forty years of practice he has never prescribed psychiatric medication to his clients except when necessary to help them withdraw from their medications. He recommends that doctors never prescribe these drugs, due to their dangerous side-effects.

Suicide Leads to Anger

My wife and I went on a cruise in 2013 and I had many opportunities to pray with people and to share this ministry with them. I spoke with two couples in the dining room who were curious about what I did. I explained how I helped people be set free from feelings of grief, anger, and shame through prayer. I asked if any of them had any grief that they would like to get rid of. One of the women said that she had a close friend who had committed suicide two months before, and she said that she still thought about it about eleven times each day. She told me that it made her angry that her friend never reached out to her or anyone before she ended her life, and she left behind four children, three grandchildren, and a new husband. Her suicide hurt all of these children and many friends, and it made this woman angry that her friend was so selfish. It also made her mad that the woman was a nurse who stole medication she injected into herself. So it was a systematic, planned suicide, and yet no one knew she was depressed or suicidal. All of this made her very angry at her friend's selfishness.

We prayed about her anger and she told the Lord why she was angry. Then she asked Him to take her anger and carry it for her. I prayed and asked the Lord if there was anything that He wanted her to know and she said, "I feel peace and it's not my fault." I asked her if she felt any anger toward her friend and she said, "No." Her anger was gone, her feelings of guilt were gone, and she just smiled and said she felt peaceful.

Suicides can profoundly impact people, leaving deep emotional scars from anger, grief, and feelings of shame, but the Lord can set us free from all of these scars and replace our pain with His peace.

Father's Suicide Resolved after Thirty Years

After speaking with a small group of Christians one evening a woman told me that her father had committed suicide thirty-three years before when she was eighteen years old. Her eyes began to redden and tears began to flow. I asked her if she would like to pray about it, and she said that she would. She allowed five others to remain in the room as we talked and prayed about her emotional pain from this tragic event that obviously still had an impact on her.

This woman said she was angry at her father for "copping out" and killing himself to avoid going to prison, she was angry that he dropped out of her life completely from age four to sixteen after her parents divorced, and he only called her when he was drunk. We made a list of twelve resentments she had toward her father and then I led her in a prayer to give her anger to the Lord. After the prayer, I asked her how she felt about her father and she said, "I have no more anger toward him; he was trying to be a dad." She then felt some sadness about how he had wasted his life, how she never got to really know him, and how he had so deeply hurt her sister. We prayed about six reasons she felt sad about him and she gave these feelings to the Lord. When I asked her again how she felt about her father she said that she felt no more sadness and she said it was "okay."

After resolving those feelings she said she still felt some shame because her father had called her on the phone just before he committed suicide. He wanted to stay on the phone, but she was in a hurry to get off, not knowing that he was planning to kill himself. She had blamed herself for his death for thirty-three years, and believed that she was a "bad, selfish person" because she didn't stay on the phone with him. I prayed and asked the Lord what He wanted her to know about those beliefs. The thought that came to her mind was, "It's all okay. I was just a teenager." These thoughts brought peace to her heart and resolved her feelings of shame. And finally, after resolving her anger, sadness, and feelings of shame she felt some grief over his loss. We made a list of eleven things she missed about him. She recalled how he was so proud of her and like to show her off to his friends, he gave her gifts, he made her laugh, and she enjoyed his sharp intellect and sense of humor. I led her in a prayer to give her feelings of grief to the Lord and she released them.

After praying through these feelings, this woman began smiling and said, "I can think of him with happiness now," and "all is well." The next day I spoke with her and she said, "It's amazing that I carried these feelings around for thirty-three years after my dad's suicide." She said that she had been "poking around" in her memories of her father and felt no more sadness, shame, or grief. She was amazed. I saw her several more times after this prayer session and she testified that she was still doing well and had no negative feelings toward her father. She even said that she found herself doing less shopping than she had previously, and she realized that she had a pattern of going shopping whenever she felt bad. The suicide death of her father at age eighteen had affected her in many ways that she had not realized, and the healing of these memories and emotions brought her many practical benefits in addition to the direct benefit of feeling better about her father.

Suicide Leads to Feelings of Shame

A pastor was referred to me when he was being discharged from a psychiatric hospital where he had received treatment for depression. His depression began when he returned home from church one Sunday morning and found that his wife had committed suicide while he was preaching at church. He was full of sadness and grief and blamed himself because he had no idea that she was depressed or suicidal. He felt that he should have known something was wrong with her. These feelings were compounded by the fact that five years earlier his son had committed suicide, so after experiencing two suicides in his family he was consumed with guilt and grief.

The pastor's doctor prescribed him some antidepressants but they did not help. He was prescribed more and stronger medications, but nothing seemed to help pull him out of his deep depression. When he continued to experience depression he was hospitalized and given a series of electroconvulsive shock treatments (ECT), and then he was released and referred to me. When I first saw him he had some memory loss from the shock treatments but he was able to function. He had returned to his other job and to his preaching, but he still had some underlying feelings of depression. I shared with him how to release his grief and shame through prayer and we began praying and releasing these feelings. Each time he returned he seemed to be doing better, until finally he stated that he no longer felt depressed and he felt that he no longer needed to be seen. I had the opportunity to see him several times after that and he stated that he was still doing well. The Lord set this pastor free from his depression, not through the psychiatric medications or through the shock treatments but through prayer.

God's Solution to Mental Illness

Our medical knowledge is far greater today than ever in the history of mankind. I had a triple-bypass ten years ago that saved my life. The medical technology that enabled me to live is remarkable. And yet our medical knowledge is very inadequate to help us deal with simple issues like the common cold and many other medical problems. But nowhere is our medical knowledge more inadequate than in the area of mental health, where doctors believe they can solve our emotional problems with a pill. The fact is that mental health professionals and doctors have found no solution for common problems like grief and anger, so they certainly cannot help with more complicated problems like depression and posttraumatic stress disorder. As shown in this book, however, the Lord is able to set us free from our grief, anger, sadness, and shame. He is able to do for us what no doctor, psychologist, psychiatrist or pill is able to do. He is able to heal us of these emotions and to replace them with His peace.

The Lord is able to heal us of depression, and since 87% of all depression is rooted in loss, we cannot help people with depression if we cannot help them with their losses. Suicides result from depression and hopelessness, but we have the God of all hope. Paul ended his letter to the church at Rome with this blessing, "Now may the God of hope fill you with all joy and peace in believing, that you may abound in hope by the power of the Holy Spirit" (Romans 15:13). May the Lord help the church today to see in Him the source of all joy and peace, and share with the world the joy and peace that come from finding emotional healing in Him.

Discussion Questions

1. Have you ever known someone who committed suicide? How did it affect you and others who knew this individual?
2. If you had a child who committed suicide, how do you think that would impact you?
3. If you had a parent who committed suicide, how do you think that would impact you?
4. Do you think that you have any continuing negative emotions as a result of a suicide? Would you like to get rid of those feelings if you could?

Personal Application

Think about someone who committed suicide that you knew personally, and identify the various feelings that you had immediately afterwards. Identify any feelings of grief, anger, sadness, or shame that you had at the time, and talk with someone about it or write out how you felt at the time. As you think about this event, observe your own emotional reactions to see if any negative emotions remain. If so, make a list of the reasons for your grief, sadness, and anger. Then talk to the Lord and ask Him to take them from you.

If you have any remaining feelings of guilt or shame, write down what makes you feel shameful, guilty, or bad. Then talk with the Lord and ask Him what He wants you to know about your belief that you should have done more, tried harder to help the person, or that you are a bad friend or family member because of what happened. Write down the thoughts that come to your mind and write down your new feelings afterwards. Continue to pray and ask for truth until you are completely free from all feelings of guilt and shame.

CHAPTER 10

Dealing with Losses
by Murder or Violence

n the previous chapter we discussed how those who lose friends or family members due to suicide often have several different emotions to resolve. The same is true for those who lose friends or family members due to a murder. Friends of murder victims usually have strong feelings of grief, anger, and shame that need to be resolved. They often need help in identifying their feelings, and you can help them with this by asking them what emotions they feel when they think about the deceased person. As they identify one emotion, continue asking what other emotions they feel, until they have all been identified. Then ask which of these emotions is the strongest, and focus on helping them resolve one emotion at a time, until all of their negative emotions are resolved.

Mothers of Murder Victims Set Free

I was invited to speak at two churches in Arkansas on a Sunday morning. At the first service I spoke about "Overcoming Grief," and at the second service I spoke about "Overcoming Anger." I agreed to pray after lunch with anyone who wanted prayer for some grief or anger, and when I returned from lunch two women were waiting for prayer. Both of these women were suffering from the trauma of having a child murdered. The loss of a child is one of the most traumatic experiences a person can have. When the child dies from violence it is even more traumatic, but the Lord is able to set us free from even the most traumatic experiences we can have.

The pastor sat in on the prayer session with the first woman and observed how she was released from her sadness, anger, and grief, and then felt peaceful and calm afterwards. She smiled and said that she felt no more anger and that she felt sorry for the murderer. What an amazing transformation! The pastor told me afterwards that it is one thing to understand this process intellectually, but it was awesome to witness it firsthand. The next day he had an opportunity to pray with this woman's sister and he said he "had a similar experience" and that it was "awesome." He was able to pray with her and see her set free after hearing two sermons and witnessing one prayer session.

I then met with the other woman, who attended the service where I spoke about grief. This woman was a patient at a nearby Christian psychiatric clinic and she was accompanied by one of the attendants. She told me that this was her third hospitalization for ten days during the last year. This began when her son was shot and killed during a robbery of a store where he worked. Although she admitted having a history of depression, she had never been hospitalized prior to the murder. She was given heavy doses of psychiatric medications to sedate and calm her, but she was still suffering emotionally from the loss of her son.

This woman explained that she had four sons, but this one was the most loving and caring to her. She lived with him twelve years when she was in need, and his death was deeply painful. I asked her what she missed the most about her son and she gave me a long list of things which I wrote down. She said he was her best friend, he supported her and took her into his home, and he was loving to her. She missed eating out with him, spending holidays and birthdays with him, shopping, fixing dinner for him, and going to church with him. She mentioned twenty-two things she missed about her son; then I led her in a prayer in which she told the Lord what she missed about him and asked the Lord to take her grief from her. I asked the Lord if there was anything He wanted her to know. She said, "I feel better," and she said she felt no more grief or sadness about her son. She reported that the following thoughts came to her mind: "He is in a better place; He is no longer in pain."

I asked this woman if she had any other negative feelings, and she told me that she was dreading going to the trial because she felt such hatred for her son's murderer. We made a short list of the reasons for her hatred and anger. Of course, she had good reasons to be angry at the murderer because he took her son's life in a senseless murder, he had a history of other crimes, and it made her angry that he had been released from jail only fifteen days before her son's murder. She stated that she would like to get rid of her anger, so I led her in a prayer as she told the Lord why she was angry and asked Him to take her anger from her. I then prayed and asked the Lord if there was anything that He wanted her to know and she said, "I know it was God's time."

After this brief prayer I asked her how she felt. She said that her anger was gone and she felt no more hatred for the murderer. She said, "I can face him now" (in the trial). She began smiling and she said she felt peaceful as she left. This example shows how powerful the Lord is and how He can set us free from our strongest emotions. The world has no solution for problems like these, but Jesus can do for us what no counselor, psychologist, doctor, psychiatrist, or medication can do. He can set us free from our negative emotions and give us His perfect peace.

Set Free from Impact of Murdered Son

At a Set Free seminar, I prayed with a woman named "Jenny". She volunteered for prayer in front of a large group of people because she was so desperate for help, and she gave me permission to share this story. Seven months earlier her 22-year-old son was murdered by a young man who was showing off for a girl. Her son lay in the street bleeding to death from a gunshot wound while the police chased down the murderer.

Jenny not only lost her son, but she attended the murder trial and was outraged at the behavior of this young murderer and his family. The murderer was crying and feeling sorry for himself because he was sentenced to eighteen years in prison, and his mother and brother were shouting out in court saying, "I love you, son" and "I love you, bro," but Jenny will never be able to hug her son again or tell him that she loves him.

I have prayed for many other people who lost loved ones through murder and there are usually feelings of grief, sadness, anger and shame. I asked Jenny what the strongest emotion was that she had, and she said she felt guilt and shame. So we focused on the shame first. Her shame was based on her beliefs that "I should have been there; I should have told him not to go to Topeka; I should have prayed more for him." So I prayed and asked the Lord what He wanted her to know. She had the thoughts come to her mind, "It's not my fault; it's ok, it's ok; he's okay." With those thoughts from the Lord she said that she felt less shame and guilt.

We talked next about her feelings of grief and she identified twenty-one things she missed about her son. She said that she missed his silliness, his helpfulness, his love for his children, talking to him, being with him, his phone calls, and his love and affection. I asked her if she was willing to give these feelings to the Lord and she was not, because she was afraid that God would test her like Job and take another child from her. I prayed for truth from the Lord but she received no truth, which usually means the person's anger is interfering. So I turned to her anger at the murderer. She was afraid that if she released her anger, the murderer would be let off the hook and she would be disloyal to her son, both of which were lies from the enemy. I prayed and asked the Lord for truth and the Lord told her, "Vengeance is Mine; let it go!" We made a list of eleven reasons for her anger but she would not give it to the Lord because she believed that if she let go of anything, "I'll lose my son." I prayed for truth and the Lord told her, "It's not true." She finally prayed and gave her anger to the Lord and then said that she felt less anger.

This process took a long time and many of the observers had to leave, so I gave them permission to go. We then focused on her feelings of sadness. She was sad because her son died so young, he left two children behind, he never fulfilled his life goals, and he and his mother had not spoken for eleven months before his death. She prayed and gave her sadness to the Lord. We had to pray twice to eliminate all the sadness, but afterwards she said she felt joy. She began smiling and said that she felt very peaceful and calm and had no more sadness. She never fully released her grief, but she did release her feelings of shame, anger, and sadness.

The following week Jenny's father died and she had to deal with another loss. But a week later she texted her friend who had brought her for prayer and said, "I feel sooo much lighter inside since praying with Jim!" She texted me several days later and told me that she was doing well. Isn't it amazing how God cares for us and bears our burdens for us? Even when we have severe traumas, like Jenny, the Lord wants us to experience His peace so that we will learn to walk with Him every day and stay close to Him

Man Releases Anger over Murder of Sister

A man came for help with his anger after being arrested for domestic violence and being ordered to receive "anger management" or counseling. He had an incident with his father when his father came to his house to help him and encourage him and he exploded with rage due to pent-up anger he had held for years. As a child he went to church and gave his life to the Lord, but when he was ten years old his mother had a severe stroke which left her unable to walk or talk and he was fearful of losing her. He resented his father for being unfaithful to his disabled mother and then divorcing her when this young man was fifteen years old, deserting her and this young man to raise himself and his siblings. At that time he was so angry that he began smoking pot, drinking beer, and getting drunk. When he was seventeen years old, his sister was murdered and he began using meth every day. After high school he joined the Army and was deployed to Iraq for one year where he was involved in combat and developed posttraumatic stress disorder (PTSD).

When he was discharged from the military he got married and his wife was very moody and jealous of him. Three years later he filed for divorce from his wife. When she refused to sign the divorce papers he grabbed her wrists and jerked the papers out of her hands, causing her to receive some paper cuts. I never read the police report on the incident to get the official version of the events, but he minimized it and denied that he had any anger problems. The court, nevertheless, ordered him to have at least six counseling sessions, so I began by collecting background information from him. He denied having an anger problem, but agreed that he had some anger toward his father, his brother, his ex-wife, and the person who murdered his sister. He also acknowledged that he had some unresolved grief over the divorce of his parents when he was fifteen years old, the loss of his sister when he was seventeen years old, and sadness over his mother's stroke and loss of health when he was ten-years-old. These three losses and four sources of anger were included on his prayer plan, and I explained how he could resolve his anger and grief through prayer. He was a little skeptical but agreed to try it and see if it helped.

We began talking about the loss of his older sister when he was seventeen years old. His older sister was a mother-figure to him after his mother suffered her stroke when he was ten years old and was disabled. He identified seventeen things he missed about his sister, and he prayed and gave his grief to the Lord. He also made a list of reasons for his sadness about his sister's murder and gave this sadness to the Lord. After this prayer he said that he felt peaceful and calm, and the following weeks he confirmed that he no longer had any sadness or grief over her death. However, he was not ready to release the anger he felt toward the man who murdered his sister and was never caught.

We talked about his father next, and he identified ten things that he resented about his father including his womanizing, the way he abandoned this man's mother after her stroke and divorced her, his drinking, and his abandonment of the children. The man prayed and told the Lord ten things he resented about his father, and then he gave his anger to the Lord. After this prayer I asked him to think about his father and tell me how he felt. He told me that he felt "happy," and he felt no more anger toward him. Several weeks later he told me that he had not been angry at his father since our last session, and he even had lunch with him. His father was so surprised at his change of attitude that he asked him if he was okay, because he was so much more friendly toward him. This man also told me that he prayed about a list of resentments he had toward his brother on his own, and he and his brother began texting every day.

We then talked about his ex-wife, and he identified eleven resentments he had toward her. He prayed and gave his anger to the Lord and asked Him to take it and carry it for him. Immediately afterwards he said that he felt calm and had no more anger toward her. I asked him how he would feel and what he would do if he met her in a convenience store in town. He said that he would probably smile at her and say "hello." A month later he told me that he was no longer angry at his ex-wife and he had not thought about her since our last meeting. He also said that his boss commented about how happy he appeared to be, and his father complimented him for not being angry at the world anymore. However, he still was not ready to talk about his anger toward his sister's murderer, so I simply encouraged him to think about how it would help him to be rid of that anger.

A month later he said that he was doing very well and had not had any more angry outbursts, and he felt no more anger toward his ex-wife, his father, or his brother. He was pleased that people could see a difference in him. He said that his brother and father got into a heated argument and he intervened calmly and was able to de-escalate the conflict between them. I asked him, again, if he would like to get rid of his anger toward his sister's murderer. He finally agreed to try to get rid of this anger and began talking about her murder.

When he was seventeen years old, his older sister was murdered outside her apartment and the murderer was never caught. There were suspicions but no one was ever arrested for the crime. This man admitted that this was very difficult for him and led to a lot of anger. He often thought about what he would to the person if he ever found out who it was. We made a list of the reasons for his anger, then I led him in a prayer and he asked the Lord to take his anger from him and carry it for him. When we were done he said that he felt "a lot better." He was peaceful and calm and did not feel any more anger toward this person.

About a year later I saw this man again. He confirmed that he was still doing well and had no more anger toward his sister's murderer. He told me that he was reading his Bible, going to church again, and he had married a Christian woman who was going to church with him. He was happy and spoke of the power of prayer and how amazing God was to set him free from the anger he once had. He was set free as we systematically prayed about each of the losses and sources of anger that had led him to be so angry.

Dealing with Posttraumatic Stress Disorder

The experience of losing a friend or loved one through murder can be classified as an example of "posttraumatic stress disorder." This is a classification that is included in the *Diagnostic and Statistical Manual of Mental Disorder of the American Psychiatric Association, Version 5* (2013), and it has been in previous versions of the DSM since 1980. Posttraumatic stress occurs any time an individual is exposed to a traumatic event such as sexual abuse, physical abuse, violence, murder, tornadoes, earthquakes, tsunamis, car accidents or any other form of natural disaster or violence. We will only briefly address such traumas here and provide an overview of the process for helping those with such traumas.

Traumas result in a variety of negative emotions, depending upon the nature of the trauma. Most commonly they include anger, sadness, shame, fear, and sometimes grief. When there is no death involved in the trauma, there is no need to deal with grief unless there is a significant loss of relationships, employment, health, property, or some other loss as a result of the trauma. When trying to help someone who has experienced a trauma, it is important to ask the person how they feel when they think about the trauma, and then help them identify the various emotional components of their trauma. After identifying their various emotions, it is helpful to ask them which emotion is the strongest, and then begin by helping them resolve that emotion. If the individual does not want to talk about that emotion, then you can begin with another emotion that is less intense, but eventually you will need to address each emotion they experienced in association with the trauma so that they can experience full healing from the trauma.

The treatment outcome research on PTSD is not very encouraging. For twenty years the Department of Veterans Affairs provided specialized programs for the treatment of PTSD for war veterans; but, after conducting studies of the efficacy of such treatments, they began to withdraw their support for specialized PTSD programs around the year 2000 due to the cost of these treatments and their perceived lack of helpfulness. Now, the treatments are mostly restricted to placing veterans on psychotropic medications and granting them disability income for the rest of their lives. It is no surprise that they cannot help individuals with PTSD since grief, anger, shame, and sadness are the primary components of PTSD and they are not able to help individuals with these emotions. But thanks be to God that He is able to set the captives free, even when they have been traumatized through their combat experiences.

Request for Help with Trauma Results in Tragedy

I met a young woman in 2013 who told me an incredible story about how psychiatric treatment for PTSD almost destroyed her. She and her husband attended a workshop that I attended in Syracuse, New York, that was sponsored by Dr. Peter Breggin, an eminent, Harvard-trained psychiatrist. I had never met this couple, but sat with them at a luncheon that was part of the conference, and I asked them what brought them to the conference. This couple was from Canada and they hesitated initially, but then this attractive, articulate young woman told me that she had experienced a trauma several years ago when someone pointed a gun at her and robbed her. She was shaken by this experience and thought she should talk with someone about it and went to a mental health clinic looking for someone to talk with about her PTSD. To her surprise, the clinic said that they did no outpatient therapy but recommended that she be hospitalized for an evaluation. Once she was admitted into the hospital she was given no counseling and was immediately placed on psychiatric medications.

The medications did not help her, but caused her to become confused and depressed. She was given more and more medications until she was deeply depressed, then they gave her multiple electroconvulsive shock treatments to relieve her of her medication-induced depression. After enduring these shock treatments she lost a lot of her mental abilities, including her short-term memory and her ability to read. She was depressed about losing so much of her mental abilities from medications and treatments, and she was understandably angry that she was damaged so badly by trusted mental health professionals. She was eventually discharged and said that she was slowly recovering from these "treatments." I had the opportunity to share with her and her husband how she could be set free from her anger and sadness through prayer. This is a shocking example of how psychiatric treatments can damage the brain and destroy lives because professionals believe that mental disorders are brain disorders or chemical imbalances.

Dr. Breggin writes openly and honestly about the dangers of psychiatric drugs and other brain-disabling psychiatric treatments being used today. In his book *Medication Madness* (2008), he tells dozens of stories about children and adults who have been emotionally damaged and sometimes driven mad or led to commit horrific crimes by psychiatric medications (Breggin, Medication Madness 2008). As a treating psychiatrist, consultant, and medical expert he has interviewed many survivors and witnesses, and reviewed extensive medical, occupational, educational, and police records on these cases. The great majority of the individuals whose cases he examined lived exemplary lives and committed no criminal or bizarre actions prior to taking the psychiatric medications.

During this conference Dr. Breggin said, "I don't think any child should ever be given a drug for their behavior or emotions." He also said, "All psychoactive substances disable your brain...and to do that to children is child abuse." I would encourage all readers to get a copy of *Medication Madness* from Amazon.com to learn how harmful these medications can be, and to realize that the answer to emotional problems is not found in psychiatry but in the Lord. Jesus is able to heal all our emotional struggles through prayer, as presented in this book. He is the answer to our problems, and He can set us free from grief, anger, shame and all of our emotional struggles because He is the Wonderful Counselor who heals the brokenhearted and sets the captives free (Isaiah 9:6, 61:1).

Jesus Heals All the Brokenhearted

Regardless of the type of loss, the Lord is able to bring complete healing to the individual as they pray and give Him their negative emotions. Loss of a person through violence and murder can be extremely traumatic and damage an individual for the rest of their life; but, as they identify each emotion they are experiencing from the traumatic event and then systematically pray about each emotion, they can be completely released from the emotional impact of the event. Whatever trauma we experience, the Lord is able to set us free and to bring complete restoration and healing to our lives. This should be very comforting to us, and give us courage to face whatever obstacles we encounter in life.

Discussion Questions

1. Do you know anyone who has lost a close friend or family member as a result of some violence, such as the terrorist attack in 2001, or as a result of murder? How did they respond to this event? Do they still struggle with their feelings about this event?

2. Have you known anyone who lost a close friend or family member as a result of a natural disaster such as a tornado, earthquake, or tsunami? Do you believe that you would know how to help such people resolve their feelings from this loss?

3. Do you have any unresolved feelings from a loss due to violence or murder that you would like to release today?

Personal Application

Think back to any losses that you have had due to violence or murder. Do you have any unresolved negative feelings regarding anyone that you knew who was murdered or who died from some form of violence? Try to identify what feelings you still have that are unresolved. Do you have any feelings of grief, anger, shame, fear, or sadness about these losses? If you still have some unresolved emotions from a murder or from violence, pray about each emotion you feel and resolve them. Share your experience with your class members and ask one of them to pray with you if you cannot completely resolve your negative feelings.

CHAPTER 11

Grief, Depression, and Medication

n Chapter 9 I described a pastor who was referred to me by his insurance provider for follow-up counseling for depression after he was discharged from a psychiatric hospital. His depression began after his wife committed suicide, which was complicated by a previous suicide by his son. He was prescribed antidepressants initially, and when they were ineffective in controlling his depression he was prescribed stronger medications, but nothing helped pull him out of his deep depression. He was then hospitalized and given a series of electroconvulsive shock treatments (ECT), and then he was released and referred to me.

When I first saw this pastor, he had some memory loss from the shock treatments, but he was able to function and had returned to his other job and to his preaching, though he still had some underlying feelings of depression. I shared with him how to release his grief and shame through prayer, and we began praying and releasing these feelings. Each time he returned, he improved a little more, until finally he stated that he no longer felt depressed and he no longer needed to be seen. I had the opportunity to visit with him several times after that, and each time he indicated that he was still doing well. The Lord set this pastor free from his depression, not through the psychiatric medications or through the shock treatments, but through emotion-healing prayer.

There is a very strong belief in our society today that all emotional and mental disorders are the result of brain disorders and chemical imbalances, and this belief was created by pharmaceutical companies as a marketing strategy for their medications (Breggin, *Medication Madness*, 2008, p. 269). Depression, substance abuse, and other mental disorders are so difficult to treat that mental health professionals have given up and simply refer these clients to psychiatrists for medications, and the psychiatrists and pharmaceutical companies are happy to provide them with medications. When I began working for one mental health clinic, I was astounded to discover that I was the only therapist trying to counsel these individuals, and my co-workers were simply referring them to the psychiatrist to receive prescriptions.

Policeman Becomes Pastor

I attended a conference where a former policeman was invited as a guest speaker to talk about his experience with "mental illness." He stated that he had worked for twenty years as a policeman, and was now a Wesleyan pastor. He described how he became severely depressed and suicidal in 1998 and was hospitalized for depression. When he was about to be discharged from the hospital he told the nurse who was wheeling him to his car in a wheelchair how he planned to kill himself when he arrived at his home. The nurse turned him around and readmitted him into the hospital for more "treatment." He was hospitalized seven consecutive times, and tried twenty different psychiatric medications, but none of them reduced his depression. He was given twelve shock treatments that left him with a lot of memory loss, but his suicidal impulses decreased somewhat.

He was stabilized on six medications, and he became a pastor and was able to function adequately for several years. Then in 2008 he was readmitted into the hospital for depression to receive more treatment due to increased suicidal impulses. After sharing this heart-breaking struggle with the audience, he concluded, "I live with mental illness every day and I have suicidal thoughts every day. I take six medications per day and will probably do so for the rest of my life." He went on to say that his depression is a brain disorder and people with mental illness need to be treated like they have a disease. He is now training police officers how to handle persons with mental illnesses.

I admired this man for his courage to publicly talk about his struggles. But when pastors, who are the spiritual leaders in our society, make such statements, it sends a message of hopelessness and conveys the idea "this is as good as it gets." As mentioned in Chapter Nine, Pastor Rick Warren returned to the pulpit four months after his son committed suicide in 2013 and spoke to his congregation in a nationally televised service. He said, "If you struggle with a broken brain, you should be no more ashamed than someone with a broken arm. It's not a sin to take meds. It's not a sin to get help. You don't need to be ashamed." It is appropriate to encourage Christians to talk more openly about their emotional struggles because James 5:16 says, "Confess your faults to one another and pray one for another" (KJV), but to say that depression is the result of a "broken brain" leads people to feel hopeless that they can ever find relief from depression.

The Bible gives a very different message, however. In Romans 15:13 the apostle Paul said, "Now may the God of hope fill you with all joy and peace in believing, that you may abound in hope by the power of the

Holy Spirit." There can be no doubt from reading the Word of God that believers are given hope that they can experience the peace of God in their lives, because peace is a fruit of the Spirit (Galatians 5:22). But we cannot have peace and be full of depression at the same time, because depression is the very opposite of peace. If we believe the Bible, we must believe that there is a way for us to experience relief from depression and have true emotional peace in the Lord.

The Relationship Between Grief and Depression

The "Virginia Twin Study," mentioned previously in Chapters One and Eight, was conducted in the late 1990s using approximately 9,000 twins in Virginia to assess the role of genetic and environmental factors in mental disorders (Kendler and Prescott 2006). Known officially as the "*Virginia Adult Twin Study of Psychiatric and Substance Use Disorders,*" this study examined twin pairs in order to differentiate the genetic and environmental influences on mental disorders that develop in adult-hood. Twins are often used when studying genetic influences, because identical twins share the same genes, so differences between the twins can be attributed to environmental influences.

In this study the researchers calculated "heritability estimates" for twenty-four mental health disorders that estimated the proportion of variation that is due to genetic factors. A heritability estimate of .50 means that if one twin has a disorder, the other twin was likely to have it 50% of the time. To understand the "heritability estimates" found for these twenty-four mental health disorders, consider the following in-herited physical conditions. Asthma, lung cancer, and breast cancer fall in the "moderate heritability range" (20-40%), blood pressure, diabetes, and heart attacks fall in the "moderately high range" (40-60%), weight and intelligence fall in the "high heritability range" (60-80%), and height falls in the "very high heritability range"(80-100%).   The researchers found heritability estimates to range from a low of 16% for social phobias and 75% for any type of drug dependence. Most mental health disorders included in this study had a heritability estimate that was below 50%, and drug dependence is the only mental health disorder that fell in the "high heritability range" between 60-80%. Although several mental disorders, such as bipolar disorders, have previously been postulated to fall in the high heritability range, more recent studies have shown them to fall in the 40-60% heritability range. None of the mental disorders examined in this study fell in the "very high heritability" range of between 80-100%.

These researchers found a very significant relationship between environmental factors such as physical abuse, sexual abuse, parental death, and parental divorce in the later development of mental disorders. Childhood abuse was found to be causally related to alcoholism and substance abuse and seven other forms of psychiatric disorders. Childhood parental death was found to be specifically related to the later development of major depressive disorders, but also increased the risk of developing a generalized anxiety disorder, panic disorder, and drug dependence. Parental divorce was found to increase the risk for major depressive disorders, general anxiety disorders, panic disorders, and substance use disorders. The risk for developing major depression, general anxiety disorders, and panic disorders as a result of parental divorce lasted for 20-35 years, and the risk for drug abuse or dependence lasted for 55 years, but the risk for alcohol dependence risk never ended. Thus, this study demonstrated a powerful connection between childhood traumas and the development of mental disorders in adulthood.

The November 2008 issue of the *American Journal of Psychiatry* reported some additional statistics from the Virginia Twin Study indicating that depressive episodes that were precipitated by life events (i.e., bereavement, divorce, illness, or job loss) accounted for 87.4% of all depressive episodes. Depressive episodes that were not precipitated by life events constituted only 12.6% of episodes in their sample. In other words, 87.4 % of the depressive episodes identified in this study of over 9,000 subjects were caused by some type of loss (Kendler, Myers and Zisook, "Does Bereavement-Related Major Depression Differ From Major Depression Associated With Other Stressful Life Events?" 2008). In their study of environmental and genetic factors affecting the development of depressive disorders, trained interviewers asked those who had experienced depression if there were any environmental events that immediately preceded the onset of their depression, and 87.4 percent of the participants indicated that they had experienced some form of loss just prior to the onset of their depression. This is an impressively high figure, and this strongly implicates the role of grief in the development of depression. This raises serious questions about the genetic and biological explanations of mental disorders, such as a "broken brain", and strongly suggests the importance of environmental factors in the development of mental disorders. This should also lead us to revise our understanding of the role of psychiatric medications in the treatment of mental disorders.

This finding is also reflected in an article written by psychologist John Rottenberg, Ph.D., in the November 2010 issue of *Psychology Today*. In his article entitled, "The Road to Depression Goes through Bereavement," Dr. Rottenberg stated that depression is closely connected to grief and loss, a finding that is not often reported among depression researchers. One must wonder how therapists and physicians, who interpret all depression as evidence of chemical imbalances or brain disorders, explain the role of bereavement in depression such as the pastor mentioned above. Did the discovery of his wife's suicide accidentally coincide with the sudden change in dopamine or serotonin levels in his brain to cause him to become depressed, or did the FACT that his wife committed suicide have some genuine, traumatic impact on his moods? The sudden loss of one's spouse has a predictable, traumatic impact on most people if they have a relatively good relationship with their spouse, and this deep grief is normal and reality-based. Placing an individual on psychotropic medications will not change the facts or take away the feelings of grief, although the medications can numb all of their feelings if the dosage is sufficiently strong.

Interestingly, Dr. Rottenberg has written a new book that was released in 2014 entitled, *The Depths: The Evolutionary Origins of the Depression Epidemic*, in which he proposes that depression is rooted in the evolution of the human species, which explains why it is so resistant to treatment. In an email that he sent out about his book he stated that the number of depressed people is growing in spite of the explosion of scientific research on depression, and the World Health Organization has predicted that by the year 2030 the amount of disability and life lost due to depression worldwide will be greater than war, accidents, cancer, stroke, and all other health conditions except for heart disease. Rottenberg wrote in his email, "In *The Depths*, I offer a new account of why depression endures—and point the way towards new paths of treatment. Drawing on recent developments in the science of mood—and my own harrowing depressive experience as a young adult—I explain depression in evolutionary terms, showing how its dark pull arises from our animal nature. Rejecting the conventional idea that depression stems from defects in the mind or brain, I show instead that sadness and depression have deep roots in our development as a species, which illuminates why mood disorders can be so tenacious."

Although I have not read this book, it is hard to imagine how such an evolutionary explanation could give us any hope for helping those with depression.

Underlying Causes of Depression

I saw a young man who drove four hours from a large metropolitan area to receive medications for his depression. He brought with him a psychological evaluation written by a psychologist who diagnosed him as depressed. The report was well written, and from my years of working closely with psychologists I could tell that the psychologist was competent and professional, but as I closely examined the report there was no indication of any precipitating factors or of the time of onset of his depression. I asked this young man when his depression began and he stated that it began at about age 18. Looking for precipitating losses I asked him if he had experienced any significant losses and he denied that he had any losses. He stated that his parents divorced when he was 17 years old but denied that this depressed him, and then he told me that his father became very depressed and began to withdraw from him, which affected him greatly since he was very close to his father. Once I had this information it was clear that the loss of his family, and the loss of his close relationship with his father, was the precipitating cause of his depression. He believed, from what he had been told by the psychologist, that his depression was the result of a chemical imbalance and not due to any environmental factors. He was only interested in taking medications to balance his chemicals.

A man was referred to me by his physician, who had attended one of my seminars. This man was deeply depressed in spite of having been on antidepressant medications for nineteen years. His depression had recently been exacerbated by the loss of his job, which he had held for twenty-seven years until the business closed. As I examined his background I learned that this man's depression began nineteen years earlier when his first wife divorced him. He had married with the intention of being married for life, and when his wife left him he became very depressed and began taking psychiatric medications. He remarried but remained depressed and dependent upon antidepressants, and then his second wife died from cancer. The same month that his wife died, his mother and father also died, which increased his depression tremendously. Four years later he lost his job, and his depression was overwhelming in spite of the antidepressants and antipsychotic medications he was taking.

I shared with this man how he could be set free from these losses through prayer, and I prayed with him first about the loss of his second wife. He was immediately released from the grief over the loss of his wife, and he went straight from our session to his wife's gravesite and felt complete peace as he thought about her. The following week we made a list of what he missed about his mother and prayed about her loss, asking the Lord to take his grief from him. His mood immediately lifted and he said he felt like going home and cleaning up the old homestead and cleaning off her gravesite. When he returned the third week he said that he mowed around the gravesite and did not feel any sadness, but he enjoyed cleaning it up and working on his parents' home. He still indicated that he had some depression, which he rated as a 3, on a 10-point scale, which had decreased from a rating of 10 since his first visit. Then we prayed about the loss of his father and the loss of his first wife, and he was able to release his grief over these losses also. Again, his mood lifted and he indicated that he felt peaceful and calm when thinking about all of these losses.

After the third visit he saw his doctor again, and his doctor was amazed at how much better he was doing. During our fourth visit, we talked about his loss of the job which he had held for twenty-seven years, and we made a list of seventeen things he missed about that job. He prayed about it and gave all his grief and sadness to the Lord, and then I asked the Lord what He wanted this man to know. He said, "He wants me to know everything is going to be okay. He is there for me;

it's going to be okay." The next time he was seen he indicated that he felt no more depression, and his doctor gradually weaned him off all his medications. I have spoken with this gentleman several times since then, and he continues to report that his depression is gone and that he is functioning well without any medications.

Creating a Prayer Plan

When dealing with individuals who have experienced a single loss, it is only necessary to help them identify what they miss about the deceased person and to assist them in praying and releasing their grief. With the man above who had depression, or when trying to help those with substance abuse or other complicated disorders, it is helpful to conduct a brief but thorough social history of the person's life to identify any underlying traumas, losses, or sources of anger. The purpose of this history is to identify all losses, sources of anger, and feelings of shame that may have contributed to the onset of their depression or other disorders, that need to be included in a prayer plan for the individual, so that they can each be dealt with.

Conducting a social history is not difficult to learn and can usually be accomplished in about an hour. A copy of a Prayer Plan Assessment Form is included in the back of this book, which may be helpful to keep beside you while you are learning to do prayer plans. I like to begin by asking questions about the person's parents and family members, to understand how their parental figures got along and how the individual got along with their parents and siblings. This can be very simple when the individual was raised by their biological parents from birth until age 18, but it can sometimes be very complicated when they are raised by a variety of parents, stepparents, grandparents, foster parents, and so forth. It is helpful to learn who raised them, how they got along with each other, and how the client got along with each of them. It is also important to find out who was raised in the same home with them, and how they got along with each of these other individuals. I also ask if they ever experienced any significant traumas, such as physical or sexual abuse, and if they experienced any significant losses before school age.

Next, it is helpful to inquire about the client's childhood and school experiences, from age five to eighteen. I ask them if they enjoyed school and ask how they did academically, socially, and behaviorally in grade school, middle school, and high school (e.g."did you make good grades, behave well, and have plenty of friends?"). If they were ever placed somewhere besides their biological parents' home, it is important to know why. I ask, again, if they experienced any significant traumas during their schooling years, or if they experienced any significant losses during these years, including romantic relationships. Many people with problematic behaviors begin to exhibit problems during their adolescent years, so it is important to ask if they ever experimented with drugs or alcohol, if they were ever arrested or in trouble at school, and whether or not they graduated from high school. If they did not graduate I like to find out why they did not.

Finally, I ask questions to learn about their adult experiences. I ask if they have ever been arrested, and if so, how many times and for what reasons. I also inquire about their alcohol or drug usage during adulthood, or whether they ever received mental health counseling, psychiatric medications, or were ever hospitalized for psychiatric reasons. It is important to find out how many serious relationships they have had as an adult, how many times they have been married, how long they were married, what type of problems they had in each marriage, and how many children they had from each marriage. Each one of these relationships is likely to have resulted in some feelings of anger or grief, or both, and this needs to be identified. Finally, I ask if they have experienced any traumas as an adult or if they have experienced any significant losses during adulthood.

This "social history" usually takes between 45 minutes to an hour because I am very directive, ask a lot of questions, and don't allow the person time to tell stories. My purpose is to gain a quick overview of the person's life events and identify the underlying feelings of grief, anger, and shame that may be affecting their life. As I gather information, I use a notation system and write a letter in the left-hand margin of the page next to any statement that suggests the person may have some anger (A), grief or loss (L), or feelings of shame (SH). When I complete the interview, I then summarize for them the possible anger issues, loss issues, and shame issues for which they need prayer, and I make three vertical lists at the bottom of the page to identify the anger, grief, and shame issues on a "Prayer Plan." If the person is interested in praying through each of these areas I like to write this prayer plan on a 3x5 card to give to them to carry so they can begin praying on their own, as they are able to do so.

Woman Set Free from Life of Depression

A woman was referred to me due to her depression which was affecting her health. She had never been on antidepressants before but admitted that she had been depressed since childhood. She was a Christian and she had a long history of significant losses, beginning at age seven when a child in her class died of a brain aneurism in the classroom. This led to a lot of sadness and depression in her childhood. After high school her boyfriend was killed in Vietnam, then she got married and her first husband died from a car wreck when she was twenty-six years old. She remarried and her second husband died from cancer. She met another man who became her boyfriend after her second marriage, and he died from cancer. She also lost her father, her mother, and a close grand-parent. All of these losses exacerbated her depression. Then her twin brother was diagnosed with cancer and she sought help for her depres-sion. These nine losses were included in her "prayer plan" for resolving her depression.

As we talked, it became clear that she was a Christian, and when I shared with her how she could be set free from her grief she was very receptive. She said that she would first like to get rid of her grief over the loss of her mother five years earlier, so she told me what she missed about her mother. She said she missed her mother's comfort and sup-port, going to church with her, her sense of humor, her cooking, her love and affection, her smile and her laughter. She also said that her mother was her best friend and she missed being with her and seeing her snow-white hair and her big brown eyes. We made a list of twenty-one things she missed about her mother, and then we prayed and she told the Lord everything she missed about her.

As she prayed, she asked the Lord to take her grief and sadness and carry it for her. Then I asked the Lord what He wanted her to know. She immediately said, "I see her smiling; I just see her smiling with her big, brown eyes." I asked her how she felt and she said, "I feel happy, no sad-ness, very calm." I asked her what she thought about this type of prayer and she said, "It's so simple! I want to help my brother with his grief over my mother." She was shocked at how quickly her grief was healed.

When she returned three weeks later she said that she had no de-pression. She said, "I feel everything is lifted off. I don't feel the urge to crawl up in bed or hide and tell people to leave me alone." This woman said that she had also prayed about some anger that she had toward a relative. She wrote down everything "ugly" that this relative had said or done and gave it to God, and then she felt sorry for her relative. She told me that she gave her sisters a copy of my grief booklet. They both wrote down their losses and gave them to the Lord, and both of them felt better. When she went into a store she saw an elderly woman with white hair and it reminded her of her mother. It just made her smile, but previously when this happened she said, "it hurt my heart." Most Tuesdays she said she was in a "black mood" because her mother had died on a Tuesday; but she said, "Now I feel good on Tuesdays and I have begun doing some visitation." She also said, "My husband is blown away! He told the men at church that he had a brand new wife. Everyone should know about this!" She still had some sadness over her brother's cancer and her father's suffering after a stroke, but she wanted to release this sadness on her own.

After the first session she stated that she no longer felt depressed, and her husband had seen such a significant improvement in her that he told their church friends that he had a new wife. We prayed about the loss of her first husband and she was able to release her grief over this loss, then she prayed on her own about some of her other losses and was able to find relief from her grief over them. When last seen she was elated and affirmed that she felt no more depression, and she was sharing with her family and friends how to be set free from grief.

Depressed Woman Set Free in Three Sessions

Another woman came to me who had been depressed for nine years since the death of her husband of thirty-five years. She had begun crying all the time, even though she had begun taking antidepressants shortly after his death, which she said numbed her feelings and stopped her crying for a time but did not take away her depression. Several weeks before we first met she began crying again, and she decided that she wanted to try to get off her medications. Together we made a list of twenty-one things she missed about her husband, and then we prayed and she told the Lord what she missed about her husband and asked the Lord to carry her sadness for her. Immediately, her sadness lifted and she felt neutral and calm while thinking about her husband, and she no longer felt like crying.

Two weeks later she said that she was no longer sad about her husband's death and that her depression was gone. We talked about her anger toward her abusive mother and made a list of fourteen resentments she had. Then she gave her anger to the Lord and asked Him to carry it for her. After praying about her anger I asked her how she felt, and she said that she felt "nothing" and had no more anger toward her mother. A month later she said that she felt "really good," and she testified that she still felt no depression and no longer had any anger toward her mother, either. We prayed about the loss of her son ten years earlier and made a list of ten things she missed about him. Then she gave her grief and sadness to the Lord and she felt peaceful about this loss.

When I saw this woman several weeks later, she stated that she was still doing well and had no depression. She said that she had no more anger toward her mother, no grief or sadness about the loss of her husband, and no grief, sadness or shame over the loss of her son. I asked her what she thought about this prayer process and she said, "I'm amazed that it worked so well!" I saw her again, a month later, and she was still doing great and affirmed that she had had no more depressive episodes and she felt good. She said, "It worked!"

Brain Disorders and Chemical Imbalances

A $20 million study was completed in 2004 called the "National Co-morbidity Study" to determine the number of Americans who experience some form of mental illness during their lifetime. Using their broad definition of what constitutes a "mental illness," they concluded that 48% of all Americans will experience some form of mental illness in their lifetime, and three-fourths of them will do so by age 24. The solution that was recommended for these disorders was that early screening and "treatment" be provided, meaning that more people be provided psychotropic medications for their "disorders."

Some researchers believe that the purpose of the study was to market psychiatric drugs for the pharmaceutical industry. Indeed, it was found in another study that over half of all individuals working on the various committees that define mental illness in the *Diagnostic and Statistical Manual of Mental Disorders* (Fifth Edition) were simultaneously employed by pharmaceutical companies, so they stood to profit financially from increased sales of psychotropic medications to those newly defined as mentally ill. The pharmaceutical industry has a strong financial relationship with the psychiatric profession and even sponsors most psychiatric conventions and conferences across the country.

Thomas Insel, M.D., the director of the Co-morbidity Study, was disappointed to learn that so many people rely upon their spiritual advisors for help with their depression, rather than upon their doctor, and said, "These are real medical and brain disorders, and they need to be treated that way." Of course, the pharmaceutical companies are in full agreement with Dr. Insel and have been promoting this viewpoint for many years. In his book, *Toxic Psychiatry* (1991), Dr. Peter Breggin documented a pact made between the American Psychiatric Association and the drug companies in the early 1970s when the APA was in financial straits (Breggin, Toxic Psychiatry: Why Therapy, Empathy and Love Must Replace the Drugs, Electroshock, and biochemical Theories of the "New Psychiatry" 1991). The board of directors of the association voted to start accepting large amounts of money from the drug companies in order to avoid going into bankruptcy, and in return the association agreed to promote the psychotropic drugs being manufactured by the pharmaceutical companies (Breggin, *Medication Madness*, p. 52).

Getting A Second Opinion: Dr. Peter Breggin

With the overwhelming support of the American Psychiatric Association and the pharmaceutical companies behind the use of psychotropic medications in treating all kinds of emotional disturbances, the average doctor has come to accept this viewpoint without question. However, it is always appropriate to seek a second opinion on important medical matters, and Dr. Peter Breggin offers a needed, well-informed second opinion. Dr. Breggin has been in private practice as a psychiatrist since 1968. In his therapy practice, he treats individuals, couples, and children without resorting to the use of psychiatric drugs. In his book *Medication Madness* (2008), he wrote, "I have always worked with the most disturbed patients without resorting to psychiatric drugs" (p. 102). Since 1964 he has authored dozens of scientific articles and written over twenty books on the adverse effects of psychiatric medications and treatments.

The FDA admitted at some hearings in 2004 that there is no substantial evidence that antidepressants are useful in treating depression in children. Dr. Breggin provides impressive evidence that these medications are not effective in treating depression in adults either. He wrote, "It's impossible to prove that antidepressants actually relieve depression but it's relatively easy to demonstrate that they can worsen depression and cause mania, murder, and suicide" (*Medication Madness*, p. 53). In 2002 a team of researchers at the University of Connecticut published a report that examined all of the studies conducted by drug companies on the effectiveness of six commonly prescribed antidepressants. Each of the six drugs had been approved by the FDA based upon two positive studies, but many other studies had previously been conducted that did not yield positive results. When these researchers examined forty-seven studies done on these six medications, they found that any positive effects were "negligible" in comparison to placebos. In 2006 another review was published in the *British Medical Journal* which analyzed the effectiveness of antidepressants such as Prozac, Zoloft, and Paxil, and concluded that these drugs "do not have a clinically meaningful advantage over placebo." However, the psychiatric and pharmaceutical communities responded to these findings by simply ignoring them and continuing with their practices and indoctrination policies in favor of antidepressant medication (*Medication Madness*, p. 53).

Not only are antidepressants ineffective, but they also pose some very serious dangers to those who take them, including the risk of causing depression, agitation, suicidality, mania, and violence. In *Medication Madness*, Dr. Breggin documents many cases of individuals who became violent or committed suicide after being placed on antidepressants, when these individuals had never previously exhibited such a risk. After a decade of ignoring Dr. Breggin's warnings about these dangers, the FDA finally placed a "black-box warning" on antidepressants in 2004. In 2007 the FDA Black Box warning was modified to say the following:

> Antidepressants increased the risk compared to placebo of suicidal thinking and behavior (suicidality) in children, adolescents, and young adults in short-terms studies of major depressive disorder (MDD) and other psychiatric disorders. Anyone considering the use of (name of drug) or any other antidepressant in a child, adolescent, or young adult must balance this risk with clinical need. Short-term studies did not show an increase in the risk of suicidality

with antidepressants compared to placebo in adults beyond age 24; there was a reduction in risk with antidepressants compared to placebo in adults age 65 or older. Depression and certain other psychiatric disorders are themselves associated with increases in the risk of suicide. Patients of all ages who are started on antidepressant therapy should be monitored appropriately and observed closely for clinical worsening, suicidality, or unusual changes in behavior.

In spite of these warnings, psychiatrists have continued to prescribe antidepressants as if there was no risk at all. Dr. Breggin has documented how antidepressants can cause people to become violent, and has evaluated many of the public acts of violence such as mass shootings in our country that have been committed in the last decade, reporting (on his website: breggin.com) that all but one of the perpetrators of such violence were already under psychiatric treatment and were taking antidepressants or other psychiatric medications that are known to have the ability to cause agitation and violent behavior.

When antidepressants are not helpful to individuals (and as has been just discussed they most often are not) doctors will often pair them with stronger drugs called antipsychotics. Television commercials advertise such drugs as Abilify and say that combining these drugs with an antidepressant may help you when an antidepressant medication is not effective by itself. But if you listen closely to the warnings given in these commercials about the adverse side-effects of these medications, it is clear that these drugs pose serious dangers to the individuals. This commercial for Abilify cheerfully explains what will happen if you take the medication:

Abilify is not for everyone. Call your doctor if your depression worsens, or if you have unusual changes in your behaviors or thoughts of suicide. Antidepressants can increase these in children, teens, and young adults. Elderly dementia patients taking Abilify can have increased risk of death or stroke. Call your doctor if you have high fever, stiff muscles, and confusion, to address a possible life-threatening condition, or if you have uncontrollable muscle movements, as these can become permanent. High blood-sugar has been reported with Abilify and medicines like it, and in extreme cases can lead to coma or death. Other risks can include increased cholesterol, weight gain, decrease in white blood cells, which can be serious: dizziness on standing, seizures, trouble swallowing, and impaired judgment or motor skills.

The warnings contained in this advertisement make it clear that this antipsychotic drug can increase depression, lead to suicide, cause uncontrollable body movements known as "tardive dyskinesia" that may be irreversible, and can even lead to death. What they don't say in the commercial is how frequently these side effects happen, and how difficult it is to get off these medications due to their serious withdrawal effects.

When psychiatric medications do not work, psychiatrists have increasingly begun utilizing electroconvulsive shock therapy (ECT), and there are very great dangers associated with this practice. Dr. Breggin was one of the first individuals who began in the early 1970s to oppose and expose the dangerous practices of lobotomies and electroconvulsive shock treatments. The practice decreased in the 1980s, but it has been revived and is being widely practiced again, in spite of the claims by psychiatrists and drug companies that we have much more effective medications now to help those suffering from depression. In his book, *Brain-disabling Treatments in Psychiatry* (2008), Dr. Breggin documents the severe disruption, memory loss, and permanent brain injury that result from ECT. I have personally worked with individuals who have undergone such treatments and they have consistently reported and demonstrated severe and permanent brain injuries. It is sad to see individuals who are so desperate for relief from depression that they will subject themselves to such measures, and it is astounding to see that mental health professionals are so ineffective in helping people with depression that they endorse such practices.

God's Ways vs. Man's Ways:

In Mark 5:21-34 Jesus was approached by a synagogue official by the name of Jairus whose daughter was very sick and was dying. Jesus began walking with Jairus toward his home and a multitude of people were following him and pressing against him, when a woman who had suffered for twelve years from a hemorrhage came up to Jesus for healing. The scriptures tell us that she "had endured much at the hands of many physicians, and had spent all that she had and was not helped at all, but rather had grown worse" (Mark 5:26) so she was desperate for relief. She had tried man's solutions and found them to be inadequate and harmful, and as a last resort she was seeking Jesus for healing.

When this woman touched His cloak she was instantly healed and "she felt in her body that she was healed of her affliction" (Mark 5:29). She tried to quietly slip away in the crowd, but Jesus turned and asked, "Who touched My garments?" And His disciples said to Him, "You see the multitude pressing in on You, and You say, 'Who touched Me?'" (Mark 5:30-31). But Jesus knew that someone had touched Him for healing because He felt the power leaving Him, and He turned to see who it was. Then the woman knew that she had been discovered by Him, and she came forward, fell to her knees and confessed that she was the one who had touched Him, and told Jesus the whole story. Jesus did not rebuke her; He simply wanted the crowds to see that His supernatural power could heal anyone and He wanted to speak with her. He said to her, "Daughter, your faith has made you well; go in peace, and be healed of your affliction."

This story is as relevant today as it was in the days when Jesus walked on the earth. Even though our medical knowledge is far more advanced, physicians are still very limited in their knowledge and abilities to help people with the many different types of afflictions that exist. Mental health professionals and psychiatrists are very poorly equipped to help people with mental issues today. Even with the most common problematic emotions, such as anger and grief, they have no solutions. When they realize after forty years of research that they cannot help people with their grief and anger, they come to the conclusion that all emotional problems are chemical or brain problems. As a result of their ineffectiveness and the profiteering of the pharmaceutical companies, most mental health professionals simply refer most of their clients for medications that disable the brain in an effort to cure the problem. When that does not work, then they resort to ECT or psychosurgery as solutions. Certainly, if you cut out enough of the brain or disable it sufficiently, the person will cease to function and will quit thinking or feeling any emotion. Just like the woman in Mark 5, many people have "spent all that [they have] and [are] not helped at all, but rather [have] grown worse."

It is astounding to consider the measures that people will take to find relief from all of their internal emotional pain. They become so overwhelmed with grief and sadness that they become immobilized or suicidal, and they are desperate to feel better. Or they are so unable to control their anger that they are willing to take medications that numb all their feelings, and they are told that they will have to take their medications for the rest of their lives. Many of these people become so disabled by their emotions that they cannot function on a job or in a marriage and they apply for disability. They feel hopeless to change their feelings and resign themselves to living with this emotional pain and with their brain-disabling medications for the rest of their lives. Sadly, even our pastors and spiritual leaders are calling these emotional problems "brain disorders" and "chemical imbalances."

The wonderful and amazing thing is that Jesus can set us free from our anger, grief, and shame very easily. Any believer can learn how to help people be set free from these emotions that are the underlying cause of most mental health problems. What a joy it is to see captives set free, to see the depressed healed, to see the grieving relieved of their grief, and to see those with anger released from the grip of their anger. Jesus is the One who heals the brokenhearted and sets the captives free, and He wants to use His people, the Church, to demonstrate His power. In the next chapter we will talk more about God's purpose for the Church and consider how He wants to display His power through it.

Discussion Questions

1. How does it make you to feel to read that Pastor Rick Warren believes that depression is the result of a broken brain? Does it make you feel encouraged?

2. Have you heard other Christian leaders talk about depression as a medical condition that requires professional attention and medications?

3. Do you know if your church or denomination has an official position on the role of medication in helping those with depression?

4. When you read stories about people being set free from depression through prayer, how does that make you feel?

5. Do you believe that the Bible teaches that believers should be able to enjoy genuine peace in their lives, even if they have experienced serious losses or traumas?

6. Have you ever experienced any depression in your life? If so, have you found freedom or do you still struggle with it? If you still struggle, would you like to be set free from depression?

Personal Application

Think back to times in your life when you may have experienced some depression. What precipitating losses did you have just prior to the onset of your depression? Try to identify all significant losses that you have had in your life and think about each one to determine if there are any unresolved losses. Make a list of all significant losses you have had, and make a list of each thing that you miss about the individuals you lost. Pray about these things and ask the Lord to take all of your grief and sadness. If you need help in completely resolving these emotions, seek help from one of your class members. Share your experiences of praying about your losses with your class members, and report to them how this affected your feelings of depression.

CHAPTER 12

No Answers in
the Churches!

When I was a teenager and observed how many Christians struggled with emotional issues, it motivated me to enter the mental health field to find answers. Although I had been taught that the Word of God had the answers to all of life's problems, I saw that there were no answers in my church to the emotional struggles of many sincere believers. I never ceased to believe that God's Word held the answers, but I knew that what was being taught in my church was inadequate in helping Christians overcome their negative feelings. I began looking for answers in the Bible and I attended a Bible college to help me broaden my search for answers, but I did not find what I was searching to find. I then began studying at secular universities and examined secular solutions by studying psychology and counseling for nine years, until I received three graduate degrees. Then I continued my search by attending workshops and professional conferences for twenty-five years looking for solutions.

After twenty-five years of experience in the mental health field I found something that actually worked, and it was a simple faith-based approach to helping people. It has been very exciting to help believers find emotional freedom through this simple prayer process, and believers continue to inform me that they found no answers in the churches. A woman drove from the southern tip of Texas to central Oklahoma in a desperate attempt to find relief from her grief and depression after losing her husband. She was excited to meet me and to learn how to release her grief and overcome her depression through prayer and she stated to me, "I found no answers in the church."

A man whom I described in an earlier chapter had been searching for a way to overcome his anger for forty years. He said that he had read the Bible extensively, memorized it, prayed, sought counsel from multiple pastors, and had gone to numerous Christian counselors, but nothing helped him resolve his anger. When he attended a Set Free meeting in Oklahoma and observed me pray with a young man who had anger toward his father, he was stunned to see how this young man was able to release his anger by simply being honest about his resentments and then praying and asking the Lord to take his anger from him. He went home that Friday evening and spent the weekend on his knees, giving his anger to the Lord, and he was set free from forty years of anger through simple prayer. He also told me, "I found no answers in the church."

Churches are in the same state today that they were in when I began this journey forty years ago. They do not teach believers how to experience emotional freedom and peace in spite of the clear claims of Scriptures that we can experience peace through the Lord, and they do not even provide an opportunity for open sharing and prayer for those in need. I became very excited about what I discovered; and as I began to try to share this with others, I found some individuals who responded immediately with an open heart and embraced the teaching. But I have also found that it is very hard to convince other fellow-Christians and pastors of what I have learned. I wrote my first book, *Trading Pain for Peace*, in 2008 and began conducting seminars in an effort to teach what I have learned from almost forty years in the mental health field; but I have discovered that there is a great deal of resistance to this teaching, especially from church leaders. I believe there are at least five reasons for this resistance from church leaders.

Lack of Practical Experience

Some good, sincere believers are resistant to this ministry because they have never been in the trenches with struggling believers and learned how greatly so many believers struggle. When you are in close contact with other believers for long you learn that even Christians who seriously attempt to follow the Lord, read His Word, know the Word of God well, and want to do what is right have serious emotional struggles at times. But if you are not deeply involved with other believers at an emotional level it is easy to believe that they are immature, lacking in faith, or not serious about the Lord when they struggle, and you can provide them some pat answers because of your "greater maturity."

Some believers get along relatively well in life, are happy, and have never been traumatized by abuse, divorce, or wayward children. and they think that if others would walk the same way they do, they would not have any struggles either. I had a good friend who was a wonderful Christian man who loved the Lord, raised some wonderful children, and was blessed with prosperity in his work. When I tried to share my excitement with him about the power of prayer to set people free, he was unresponsive. He didn't understand what I was sharing or appreciate it, because he had never experienced any serious emotional struggles himself. He believed that if everyone shared his doctrinal beliefs they would simply trust the

Lord with their problems and would be free of anxiety, anger, and emotional distress. He had lived a sheltered life with good parents and had never experienced any significant traumas, so he did not know how to deal with people with depression, addiction, or marital problems. He was confident that all anyone would need to do is trust the Lord.

I was sitting in a room waiting for an appointment I had with the director of a Baptist association to talk with him about my ministry. While waiting I had a nice conversation with the secretary about my ministry, and when I told her how the Lord is able to help people with their grief and anger, she was very receptive and interested in what I had to say. We were having a wonderful conversation and she shared some experiences that illustrated the prayer principle I had shared with her. It was obvious that these personal experiences enlightened her and enabled her to understand the importance of this ministry.

Then a young man entered the room and sat down. He was also there to see the director, who was running behind on his schedule. I continued my conversation with the secretary about the power of the Lord to help Christians struggling with their emotions, and this young man jumped into the conversation and began stating, confidently, that such people are in rebellion to the Lord and need to be confronted with their rebellion and lack of faith. I engaged in a brief discussion about the Scriptures and tried to share some insights that I had acquired through my study of the Bible and through my thirty-five years of experience, but this young man was certain that believers who have emotional issues are guilty of some sin or are living in disobedience. As we were talking I came to realize that this young man was a pastor and was closed-minded and dogmatic in his convictions about the emotional and spiritual needs of believers due to his youthfulness and lack of experience in trying to help believers. It was sad to consider the damage that he probably brought to his congregation due to his lack of experience.

Professional or Personal Pride

It is difficult for those who have devoted many years of their life to studying psychology or counseling to have an open mind to this ministry. Professional mental health counselors, whether they are Christian counselors or secular counselors, take pride in their profession and gain some self-esteem and status in the eyes of others due to their profession. Others seek out their advice and assistance in dealing with life difficulties due to their education and professional credentials, and this makes them feel superior to others. When someone, like me, makes statements that challenge their beliefs and the value of their profession, they are prone to react and become defensive of their profession. As I have tried to share my discovery with other Christian mental health professionals that I am seeing people resolve emotional and psychological issues through prayer, this sounds simplistic and childish to them and they quietly disregard me and avoid me. Christian counselors have difficulty accepting such claims; even those who believe in the Bible and prayer and appear to be strong Christians. But to accept such teachings and to believe that Jesus is the only answer to our emotional needs is very threatening because it threatens their livelihood, and they become concerned about losing their professional license if they begin praying with clients.

I understand these concerns because I went to nine years of college in order to learn how to help people with their emotional issues. If I had encountered someone during the first ten years of my professional life who told me that all mental health problems could be resolved through prayer, I might have been skeptical as well. I knew that something was missing in the teachings of the church, because I had observed sincere believers for ten years of my life as a child and I knew there were no answers in the church for emotional problems. I went to college looking for answers and I knew that some secular approaches were unbiblical and could not help people, but I was looking for something that did work. But after being in the profession for twenty-five years I came to realize that I was not able to help people with the most common issues experienced by individuals, such as anger and grief. I was open to learning something new that was more effective, and when I first heard about a prayer-based approach to emotional healing it made sense to me biblically and psychologically. I was not defensive about my education or worried that I had wasted my time studying for my career; I just wanted to find some way to truly help others.

Secular psychology and counseling have so many different theories and counseling models that it was obvious, as I studied, that there was no accepted approach to helping people, and that professional mental health therapists were confused about how to help people with emotional problems. There are many different counseling theories, over 250 models according to Raymond Corsini, author of the standard counseling theories textbook, *Current Psychotherapies* (Peacock, 1989, p. 9), and it takes a lot of time to sort through these different theories and to decide which one works best for each individual counselor. Corsini wrote, "If we examine various theories and procedures in psychotherapy, we find a truly bewildering set of ideas and behaviors, some of which appear quite bizarre" (Corsini, p. 1). Each new counselor goes to college to learn these different approaches and then has to make a personal decision about which one makes the most sense to them, and to develop their own personal model.

To further complicate matters, there are researchers who claim that their approach is more "evidence-based" than others in an attempt to get others to endorse and follow their approach. The difficulty is that there is so much contradictory research into treatment outcomes that even the experts cannot agree about what works best. The results of their research are hidden behind statistical concepts that most therapists do not understand, so the average clinician believes that there are more effective techniques that they need to learn, and they continue going to seminars and conferences in the hope that they will eventually find effective approaches. When someone like myself states that a simple prayer-based technique is more effective than all the techniques they learned in graduate school, it is threatening to them.

Not only does professional pride prevent some people from accepting this ministry, but there are many pastors and Christians who have personal pride that prevents them from accepting it, also. Pastors and church leaders are imperfect humans and they struggle like the rest of us. The Bible is clear that pride interferes with the ability of many people to hear the truth. Jesus spoke only the truth, but it offended some. However, the multitudes who followed Him did so because they recognized that He was speaking the truth, and they said, "Never did a man speak the way this man speaks" (John 7:46). Some pastors feel that they must have superior understanding of all matters because of their leadership position in the church, and they are not receptive to new insights offered by members of their congregation or by outsiders. And yet most of them will admit that they are not trained to deal with mental disorders and are quick to refer their parishioners to secular counselors for their emotional and mental health issues.

Jesus had many encounters with the Pharisees and religious leaders during his lifetime, and He often confronted them about their pride. He warned His disciples that they would be persecuted and rejected, because He was their teacher and leader and He was rejected and persecuted. When He sent out the seventy disciples to go before Him in pairs to every city, He forewarned them that some people would receive them and some would not. He also gave them instructions on how to respond to those who did not receive them. He said, "Whatever city you enter and they receive you, eat what is set before you; and heal those in it who are sick, and say to them, 'The kingdom of God has come near to you.' But whatever city you enter and they do not receive you, go out into its streets and say, 'Even the dust of your city which clings to our feet we wipe off in protest against you; yet be sure of this, that the kingdom of God has come near.' I say to you, it will be more tolerable in that day for Sodom than for that city" (Luke 10:8-12). The same advice could be given to those who seek to spread the truth that Jesus can truly heal the brokenhearted and set the captives free (Isaiah 61:1). Many believers will reject you due to their hardness of heart.

Personal Struggles

Many Christians are resistant to Emotional Healing Prayer because of their own personal struggles and their fear of thinking about their feelings or talking with others about their internal struggles. There are so many believers and pastors who are already taking psychiatric drugs and are embarrassed to admit this. They have been indoctrinated by their doctors to believe that all of their problems are due to chemical imbalances or brain disorders. Psychiatric medications are a big business and there are approximately 200 billion prescriptions filled in the U.S. every year. It is estimated that about 25% of all Americans are taking some type of psychiatric medication and the pharmaceutical industry is continuing to try to expand their market to have more children on psychiatric drugs. It is no different in the average church; about 25% of everyone sitting in church is taking a psychiatric drug for some reason, including the pastors.

I saw a client while writing this chapter who came seeking help with his anger. He was a Christian man who spoke openly about the Lord and wore a baseball cap with a Christian message embroidered on it. He told me that he had struggled with his anger a long time, and he admitted honestly that he had slapped one of his children so hard that he left a mark on her face, and this child had been removed from his custody for six months. That incident had happened several years earlier and he admitted that he was wrong for doing this, but he was still getting angry at his children and he wanted help with his anger. He told me that his pastor recommended that he talk with someone about taking some medications for his anger, because the pastor also had a problem with anger and he took some medications and it helped him. I visited with this gentleman and learned about his history: he grew up in a home with an alcoholic, violent father and he had been hurt by several other people. I shared with him that medications can numb all of his feelings but they cannot get rid of the underlying anger. I met with him later to help him get rid of his anger through prayer.

In nearly forty years of experience as a mental health professional I have met many mature Christians and pastors who have serious problems with anger, depression, and every other type of mental disorder. Like the pastor who recommended this Christian man seek some type of medication to help him with his anger, many pastors are already taking psychiatric medications including antidepressants, mood stabilizers, and anti-psychotic medication; and they are not eager to share this with their congregations. They also become very defensive and resistant when they hear me say that the Lord can set us free from our anger, grief, shame, and fear through prayer. They don't want to even talk about this subject for fear that their emotional struggles will be exposed. This is one of the reasons for such strong resistance to this ministry.

Media Indoctrination

As discussed in the previous chapter, there has been a strong effort on the part of the pharmaceutical industry to teach us that our emotional struggles are the result of brain disorders and chemical imbalances, and they have done an excellent job of spreading this belief. Dr. Breggin states in *Medication Madness* (p. 214), "The promotional efforts of drug advocates have been phenomenally successful." Through advertisements and television shows everyone talks as if they are mental health experts, and have come to believe in the chemical imbalance theory of depression, and to believe that only medications can help those who are psychologically disturbed. There is hardly a day that goes by in which I do not hear a Christian talk about bipolar disorders and depression as if it is an established fact that they are the result of brain disorders or chemical imbalances that can only be helped through the use of medications. Very few people, including pastors and strong Christians, have even questioned this assumption, or have any idea how these very medications are responsible for much of the unprovoked violence in our society.

While writing this chapter I had an elderly woman referred to me for counseling because she had a cousin who shot herself in the head and committed suicide. Her cousin was a very talented musician and song writer, and it was very disturbing to this woman that she had killed herself. When she went to see her doctor the next day, the doctor told her that she was depressed and needed to be on an antidepressant, so the doctor wrote out a prescription for an antidepressant. When I saw this woman the next day I asked her how she felt and she told me that she was feeling much better because her church friends had prayed for her. I asked her if she felt any sadness and she said that she felt a little sadness, which she rated as a 2, on a 10-point scale. I explained to her how she could release that sadness through prayer and asked her if she would like to try that. She said that she would, so I made a list of four things that made her sad about her cousin, and then I led her in a prayer to give her sadness to the Lord. When we were finished I asked her how she felt. She said that her sadness suddenly lifted and she felt completely peaceful and had no more sadness.

I talked with this woman about her medications and asked if the doctor had warned her about the potential adverse side-effects of the medication. She said that the doctor had not warned her of any possible side-effects, and the pharmacy had not provided her a written list of side-effects, either. I looked up her medication on a medical website and read to her some of the possible side-effects including depression, suicidality, confusion, aggression, violence, and hallucination. This elderly woman was shocked and told me that she didn't think she was depressed and she didn't want to take any medication, but her doctor convinced her that she was depressed and she needed to take an antidepressant. This doctor was negligent on a number of levels. First, the doctor was ill-informed about depression and should never have diagnosed this woman as depressed one day after she lost a close relative. The woman was experiencing normal bereavement and not depression. Second, the doctor should have informed her about the potential adverse side-effects of the medication because the risks are very serious. Third, doctors cannot tell their patients how they feel and recommend patients to take an antidepressant when they say they are not depressed. Doctors are not experts in everything and most of them have no knowledge of mental health issues or emotional problems. Most of them do not even understand the serious, harmful side-effects of the psychiatric medications that they prescribe.

This woman was a Christian, but she was easily persuaded by her doctor to take an antidepressant that she did not need and that could potentially harm her seriously. Believers in all churches need to be taught by their pastors that Jesus is the answer and that He can enable us to have true peace and joy, and that peace cannot be found in a pill. Christians need to strike from their vocabularies words like "chemical imbalance," "bipolar disorder," and "ADHD," and come back to a biblical view of emotions. They need to be taught and to understand that secular therapists are powerless to help them resolve feelings of grief, anger, or shame. Jesus can resolve these underlying emotions behind almost all types of so-called "mental disorder."

Fear of False Teaching

In every church there are individuals who act as the guardians of their church doctrine, and who are looking for erroneous teaching to oppose. Certainly, the Scriptures warn us to be on guard for false teachers. The apostle Paul left Timothy behind in Ephesus and wrote to him to "instruct certain men not to teach strange doctrines" (1 Timothy 1:3). He also wrote to Titus and instructed him to appoint leaders in the church at Crete who were "able both to exhort in sound doctrine and to refute those who contradict" (Titus 1:9). When Paul was traveling as a missionary and establishing churches, he came to the city of Berea and entered the synagogue of the Jews to preach about Jesus. The Scriptures tell us that "these were more noble-minded than those in Thessalonica, for they received the word with great eagerness, examining the Scriptures daily, *to see* whether these things were so" (Acts 17:11). These believers were commended because they cautiously examined Paul's teachings, but once they had examined the Scriptures they found that what he taught was consistent with the word of God and many of them believed. New teachings must be carefully examined to see if they are consistent with God's word, but we must not be so anxious and fearful that we miss important truths that the Lord wants us to know.

I was excited when I first began sharing with others how to find emotional freedom through prayer, and a young man who was a leader in his church became excited about the teaching and held a video conference in his church. He attended a church that was planted by a well-known Christian musician, and I was excited at the prospect that this might be the first church in the area to embrace this prayer ministry and help spread it. About ten people from his church attended the seminar and seemed to be responsive to it; but, a few weeks, later the Christian musician asked him not to promote it any more, because his mother-in-law believed that it was based upon some false teaching. There were no specific biblical concerns expressed but just a general feeling that this prayer ministry was something new and could not be from the Lord. The entire church suffered as the result of one woman who felt vaguely uncomfortable with the ministry, even though it is simple prayer and teaches that the Lord can set us free. Perhaps this elderly woman was taking psychiatric medications already and did not want to hear that she could be set free from her emotional struggles through prayer alone.

A woman came to one of my seminars and was struck with the Scripture, "Come to Me, all who are weary and heavy-laden, and I will give you rest" (Matthew 11:28). She had lost her husband of 40 years and was deeply hurting still, so she attended a Set Free meeting and I prayed with her and saw her set free from her deep grief and sorrow. She was so excited that she invited me to do a presentation at a Bible study in her home, and about thirty people attended. I did a prayer demonstration with a woman who had just lost her husband nine days earlier and this woman was immediately set free from her grief and shame. I was excited because many believers from this woman's church were present to observe, including the pastor of her church. She then organized a seminar to be done at her church and she advertised it in the local newspaper. I was hopeful that this might be the first church to embrace this prayer ministry and spread it. The seminar was poorly attended and the following day one of the elders of the church, a physician, preached at this church and stated that "you cannot just give your anger or grief to the Lord." She was shocked at the response of this church leader and decided that she may have inadvertently offended the church leaders by organizing the seminar without their approval. This church never embraced this ministry in spite of this woman's powerful testimony to her own deliverance, and the witness of the woman who had been set free from her grief over the loss of her husband nine days earlier. It just takes one church leader with underlying emotional issues to prevent an entire church from benefiting from this ministry.

I did a seminar in another state and a man volunteered for prayer. He had gone through a divorce in the preceding year, and during the prayer session his emotions were released as he broke down in tears over the deep sorrow he experienced in losing his wife. When we were finished he was able to smile and talk about his ex-wife without any anger or grief, and I spoke with him several times the following year. He even organized a seminar at his church the following year and was still excited about the ministry, but another one of his church leaders was in attendance at the seminar who had some misgivings about the ministry. This other man began doing some research online and found some critics of the prayer ministry from which I had learned these prayer principles, and came to some erroneous conclusions about it. He convinced the other leaders of their church that my ministry was not biblical and did not teach the need for repentance, which is not true. In spite of the first man's miraculous and immediate healing of his grief, the ministry was never embraced by this church due to one man's misguided feelings about it. Once again, the ministry was resisted by spiritual leaders who had some underlying emotional issues that prevented them from being able to be open-minded to the truth. These leaders resisted this simple teaching that could have set their entire church free from emotional bondage, in order to be able to serve the Lord and bring glory to Him.

Those who have deep, underlying feelings of fear, jealousy, or some other emotion can react to the simple concepts of Emotional Healing Prayer and reject it. If those individuals are influential members of their church they may prevent this ministry from being integrated into their church. Jesus experienced such rejection by many of the Jewish leaders, especially those from his hometown who "took offense at Him," where He did very few miracles due to their unbelief (Matthew 13:57). Likewise, the Jewish leaders in Thessalonica were jealous and "stirred up the crowd" (Acts 17:8) and drove Paul and Silas from their city. But they were met by the Bereans who were "more noble-minded" and who "received the word with great eagerness, examining the Scriptures daily," and "many of them... believed" (Acts 17:11-12). In order for this simple, powerful teaching to be accepted into churches to begin transforming their lives, it will be necessary for the influential members of the church to be like the Berean believers who responded without fear or jealousy to the promptings of the Holy Spirit.

God's Plan for the Church

Jesus came to heal the brokenhearted and set the captives free. When Jesus was crucified and resurrected, the Church began to carry forth this mission to the world. In the early New Testament Church, people were excited about the Lord and seeing radical transformations in the lives of new believers as the Holy Spirit filled them and the Church grew exponentially. There is much evidence in the book of Acts and in the New Testament epistles that they were seeing miracles on a regular basis, as people were being healed of physical problems, and they were experiencing victory in their personal lives as they regularly prayed with one another and cast all of their cares upon the Lord. The apostle Paul wrote to the church at Galatia that "the fruit of the Spirit is love, joy, peace..." (Galatians 5:22), and we're told in Acts13:52 that the disciples "were continually filled with joy and with the Holy Spirit." In spite of being persecuted they were not depressed, anxious, or angry, like believers are today. They were full of joy and peace.

Christianity radically transformed the dark world that existed in the times of Jesus and led to the halting of infanticide, the abolition of slavery, the emancipation of women, the establishment of hospitals, orphanages, and schools, and many other social benefits that we enjoy today in the United States. Alvin J. Schmidt documents these influences in his book, *How Christianity Changed the World* (Schmidt 2004). Jesus spoke in the Sermon on the Mount about the darkness of the world when He said, "If, therefore, the light that is in you is darkness, how great is the darkness!" (Matthew 6:23). When the influence of Christianity is removed from our society and world, it becomes very dark, indeed.

Throughout the centuries the church has been a bright beacon of light in the dark world. As the Church grew and prospered, societies were blessed and prospered; and as the Church grew lukewarm or cold, the society became more darkened and despairing. When revivals have occurred from time to time, God's people have turned back to Him and spread the truth about His redeeming love and grace. The Church has always been the beacon of light to the world and has carried the truth to the masses in our societies.

The United States has gone through several periods of spiritual revival and spiritual decline. Around the first of the twentieth century, doctors and psychiatrists began to treat those with mental health problems. Sigmund Freud was a "mechanistic deterministic thinker" who began to offer misguided solutions to the emotional problems of people in our society, that were devoid of any biblical concepts. Although his family was Jewish, he was an atheist who believed that religious beliefs were delusional (Corsini 1984). Churches were initially resistant to these new voices; but, since they failed to address the emotional issues of their hurting members, the influence of these secular psychotherapists grew over the years.

During the middle of the twentieth century Christian counselors and psychologists began to surface, offering some alternatives to the secular theories; but, they mostly mimicked the teachings of the secular therapists and failed to offer any truly meaningful alternatives. Somewhere over the last twenty centuries the Church got away from the basic practices of the early New Testament Church of praying for one another, casting their cares upon the Lord, and praying for truth to set them free. Churches are now living under the complete domination of a hopeless biological model of human needs that has led to many of their members becoming dependent upon ineffective and harmful medications, electroconvulsive shock treatments, and psychosurgery. Approximately 25% of the members of our churches are taking psychiatric medications due to the lack of biblical teaching on how to overcome negative emotions and find victory and peace in Christ. There is very little evidence of radical transformation in the lives of believers today, and it is no wonder that church attendance continues to decline.

Taking Back the Responsibility

The Church has become irrelevant to the emotional needs of individuals, and has become a place where believers congregate for an hour a week, sing songs for twenty minutes, and then hear a thirty minute sermon that is somehow supposed to provide them the sustenance, guidance, encouragement, and teaching they will need to live victoriously the rest of the week. There is very little genuine fellowship, and it has become increasingly difficult to find a church that even prays. Those that do pray generally just pray for those in their congregation who have cancer or other serious medical problems. The Church desperately needs to step up to the challenge of addressing the mental and emotional needs of those in our churches and those outside the Church.

There are several things that need to happen for the Church to become relevant to the emotional needs of people and to begin helping those with emotional and mental problems. First, the Church needs to teach these simple prayer principles publicly and frequently, so that the congregation knows that there is a way to overcome emotional problems and that it is not God's will for us to be stuck in our negative emotions. It should not be a great leap for churches to begin teaching more about the importance and power of prayer and, as part of this teaching, to teach the two simple prayer processes taught by this ministry. The first principle is based upon 1 Peter 5:7, to cast all our anxieties upon Him, by specifically identifying the specific reasons for our anger, grief, sadness, and disappointment, and then giving them to the Lord. The second principle is based upon James 1:5, to ask for wisdom from God and allow Him to bring truth to us to set us free from belief-based feelings like shame, fear, helplessness, and hopelessness.

Churches spend a great deal of time teaching doctrine and Bible truths to their members and providing them with important information about the Lord. This truth is important, and Jesus Himself spent a lot of time teaching His disciples and the multitudes, but He also took His disciples aside and taught them experiential truths through life experiences. This is very important, because our emotions are not learned through didactic teaching in a classroom or from reading a book, but through life experiences. This is why Jesus spent all day teaching the multitudes and His disciples in Mark 4 and then got into a boat with them and went to sleep. He wanted to teach them experientially how to deal with fear, so He went to sleep and allowed them to struggle with their fears as a storm arose and began to fill their boat with water. They finally awakened Him and cried out for help, and He spoke to the wind and the waves and said, "Peace, be still" (Mark 4:39, KJV). They learned experientially that the Lord could take care of them in all situations, and that it was their internal lies that made them fearful. They believed that Jesus didn't care, that they were going to die, and they didn't know that He was the Creator. Churches need to move beyond their didactic teachings and teach their members how to give their feelings to God, or to ask for truth to be set free from their emotional bondage.

Second, every new believer needs to be discipled and taught how to overcome negative emotions so that they can live victoriously and overcome sin in their lives. All believers struggle with sin and need to be taught shortly after their conversion to confess their sins to the Lord when they fail, and then learn how to identify the underlying reasons for their failure so that they can be set free and not live in a cycle of continuous defeat. Feelings of anger lead to sin and give the devil an opportunity, according to Ephesians 4:26-27, and other unresolved feelings like grief and shame can do the same. Because the Church fails to teach this principle clearly and frequently, many believers struggle with sin. This leads them to believe that they are not truly saved, so they repeatedly ask Jesus into their heart. Even those who are clear about their salvation struggle with sin and need to be taught to daily give their anger, grief, and shame to the Lord so that the devil does not have an opportunity in their lives to rob them of the joy and peace that the Lord wants them to enjoy.

Third, the church needs to provide an opportunity for members of their congregation to interact in a meaningful way and to talk about their feelings, so that they can pray for one another (James 5:16) and "bear one another's burdens" (Galatians 6:2). This cannot be done in the context of a typical worship service or Sunday School class where the focus is on studying the Bible and learning basic doctrine and truth. It is important for believers to become grounded in the Word of God, so this should not be replaced, but it is also very important for them to be involved in intimate, redeeming, healing relationships where they are able to pray honestly and meaningfully with one another. Most churches do not encourage this type of personal sharing and prayer in their Sunday School classes, and most Christians are strongly resistant to the idea of talking about their personal problems with others in their church and Sunday School classes. This could be done in "small groups" that are designed for this purpose, or it could be done in weekly prayer meetings where individuals meet in small groups so that they can pray about their personal issues.

However, meeting together with a small group or a prayer group for one hour per week is not going to be adequate for addressing the massive prayer and emotional needs of the church members. When you examine the pattern of the early New Testament church in Acts it is apparent that they met "day by day" and "from house to house" (Acts 2:46) and they "were continually devoting themselves to prayer" (Acts 1:14, 2:42, Romans 12:12). Every Christian has struggles and needs prayer from other believers at times, and it is impossible to have this type of intimacy in a typical twenty-first century church where there is a one-hour "worship" time in which you spend thirty minutes singing and thirty minutes listening to a message from God's Word while looking at the back of the heads of your fellow-believers. The Church must break out of this cultural stereotype and facilitate the development of intimate relationships and spend much more time with one another if we are going to see our churches set free.

If churches restructure and allow time for such intimate prayer groups in their weekly activities, the members will also need to learn the importance of listening to one another and being "quick to hear, slow to speak *and* slow to anger" (James 1:19). Christians in these fellowship groups also need to learn how to "clothe yourselves with humility toward one another" (1 Peter 5:5), "speak... the truth in love" (Ephesians 4:15), "rejoice with those who rejoice, and weep with those who weep" (Romans 12:15), and "devot[e] themselves to prayer" for one another (Acts 1:14, 2:42). There are many instructions given in the New Testament for how believers should relate to one another and care for one another. The New Testament Church pattern allows Christians to genuinely pray for one another in an intimate and personal way, and shows that the early Church knew how to help one another overcome feelings of grief, anger, and shame and enjoy peace, even in the midst of persecution (See Acts 13:52). We need to return to this pattern in order to see Christians experiencing joy, peace, and victory without turning to mind-altering drugs to deal with their emotions.

Creating an Army of Prayer Ministers

If all of the mental health professional counselors in the world were suddenly converted and trained to help others through a prayer-based counseling approach, there would still not be enough of them around to handle the massive numbers of emotional needs in our world. What is needed is not to train mental health counselors how to effectively help people, but for churches to be willing to take back the responsibility of equipping every believer to learn how to pray effectively about their own emotions so that they can walk in victory.

Those who wish to learn how to pray effectively with others for their emotional healing can learn to do so in far less time than it takes to go to college and get a degree. I offer a training program that includes three four-hour seminars, ten hours of personal prayer ministry, ten hours of observation of prayer ministry sessions, and ten hours of video observation and discussion. This amounts to approximately forty hours of training to have the basic skills necessary to begin doing this prayer ministry.

Those who complete these basic requirements will then be eligible to have their name added to my website, tradingpain.com, as a prayer minister in their city, and others can seek prayer ministry through them.

Of course, it takes more time to learn how to actually apply these principles to the large variety of emotional problems that exist, but this is the basic training program for starting to use this ministry, and it is offered free of charge. I know many people who are effectively helping others through this prayer ministry who have never taken a psychology course or gone to college, and they are helping people with anger, grief, shame, sexual abuse, addiction, depression, and PTSD. Most mental health therapists will just refer such patients to a doctor for medications and not even attempt to do therapy with such patients, because they have never seen anyone healed of any of these problems. And yet, I see prayer ministers whom I have trained who are effectively ministering to such people every day.

One man, a close friend in my church, began attending my Sunday School class and observed me as I prayed with several people. He began to pray for his own healing and then began praying with his wife and children and has become very competent as a prayer minister. We minister together in the jails with individuals with serious anger, sexual abuse, grief, and addiction problems, and he does an excellent job of helping people with serious problems. This man has never taken a psychology course, and yet he is helping people with serious problems that most mental health professionals try to avoid due to their complexity.

A woman in Tennessee has been a strong supporter of this ministry for many years, since she read *Trading Pain for Peace* in 2008 and attended one of my training seminars in Tennessee. She does a lot of ministry over the phone and has been very effective in praying with people with serious traumas, losses, and anger problems. She has used this process effectively for herself and her family and seen a lot of dramatic, powerful emotional healing through her prayer ministry, and yet she has no formal training in counseling. The Lord is using her mightily through her knowledge of this ministry.

A youth minister in Kansas has been using this prayer ministry since 2011 and has effectively ministered to many youth and adults in his community. He has responsibility for the spiritual care of many youth workers who are ministering to approximately 200 young people in his county. He is very competent and effective in using this ministry, but has never taken any college classes or studied counseling or psychology. When we have opportunity to visit I am amazed at the testimonies he shares about how the Lord has set many people free who have experienced severe traumas or who have serious disorders that mental health professionals are unable to help. The Lord is using this man to set many captives free, and he has spread this through his networking and relationships with other youth ministers in his area.

What God is doing through these three individuals He wants to do through an army of prayer warriors who are equipped to help those suffering from emotional problems in our churches. The secular world has no answers for even the simple emotional issues of grief, anger, and shame, so they have concluded that these are all symptoms of brain disorders and chemical imbalances. The psychiatric profession and pharmaceutical companies have been in league since the 1970s to convince the world that they need medications that are doing more harm than good and damaging many people, including Christians who believe their doctors that they need pills to find freedom.

Demonstrating the Power of God

"No answers in the churches" is the title of this chapter, but the answers are found in the Word of God and in effective, emotion-healing prayer.

The mandate is clearly given to the church in James 5:16, "Confess your faults one to another, and pray one for another, that ye may be healed" (KJV). There is a tremendous need for the church to step up to the challenge of demonstrating the power of God to set people free from emotional bondage. This needs to begin in the Church as church leaders get set free and begin teaching their members how to find freedom from grief, anger, shame, fear, addiction, depression, and traumas. As more and more individuals in their churches find freedom and begin to spread this message of hope and freedom, they will encounter opposition from within the Church and from those outside the Church. But the freedom that will come to believers in the Church and to the entire Church will be a clear contrast with the bondage that is found in the world's solutions, and many people will be drawn to the Church because of the dramatic evidence of God's power.

In 1 Kings 18 the prophet Elijah went to meet with the wicked king Ahab on Mt. Carmel to have a confrontation with Ahab and the false prophets of Baal. God had withheld rain from Judah for three years and six months, in response to the prayers of Elijah, but then God told him to meet with Ahab on Mt. Carmel. When they met, Elijah spoke to the Israelites and said, "How long will you hesitate between two opinions? If the Lord is God, follow Him; but if Baal, follow him" (1 Kings 18:21). He proposed that he and the priests of Baal both erect an altar and place a sacrifice on their altar and cry out to their god to send fire from heaven to ignite a fire for their altar. He said that the god who responds and sends fire from heaven is the true god and he would follow whichever one was the true god. They all agreed that this was a good idea, so Ahab's prophets of Baal built their altar and placed their sacrifice on the altar and began to pray and cry out to their gods. All day long they prayed and shouted and cried out to their gods to send fire from heaven but nothing happened. Elijah began to mock them and told them to cry out louder because their god might be sleeping or be on a journey. The prophets of Baal leaped around the altar and beat on themselves and cut themselves but it was all in vain. No fire came from heaven to light their altar, and so as the evening came near Elijah stepped forward.

Elijah had some faithful believers in the LORD help him build an altar and place a sacrifice upon it. Then he ordered them to dig a trench around the altar and pour twelve large clay pots of water on the sacrifice so that it was thoroughly drenched with water. He wanted to make sure that there would be no false accusations of trickery or spontaneous combustion. He then lifted his eyes to heaven and prayed the following prayer:

> O LORD, the God of Abraham, Isaac and Israel, today let it be known that Thou art God in Israel and that I am Thy servant and I have done all these things at Thy word. Answer me, O LORD, answer me, that this people may know that Thou, O LORD, art God, and *that* Thou hast turned their heart back again. Then the fire of the LORD fell and consumed the burnt offering and the wood and the stones and the dust, and licked up the water that was in the trench. And when all the people saw it, they fell on their faces; and they said, The LORD, He is God; the LORD, He is God. (1 Kings 18:36-39)

James, the brother of the Lord Jesus, challenges us to consider the example of Elijah and to "confess your sins to one another, and pray for one another, so that you may be healed. The effective prayer of a righteous man can accomplish much" (James 5:16). He tells us that "Elijah was a man with a nature like ours, and he prayed earnestly that it might not rain, and it did not rain on the earth for three years and six months" (James 5:17 Then "he prayed again, and the sky poured rain, and the earth produced its fruit" (James 5:18).

We are living in a day and age similar to the times of Elijah where we are surrounded by those who are following false gods. But the Lord wants to demonstrate His power to the world and to see His people turn back to Him. He has given us the incredible power of prayer to demonstrate to the world that He alone is God. He alone can heal the brokenhearted and set captives free from grief, anger, shame and addiction. I tried my best for twenty-five years and failed, and the world has tried its best and has failed, and now it is time for the Church to step up and demonstrate His power through prayer. As each of us learns to pray effectively, the world will respond the same way that the witnesses did in Elijah's day and fall to their knees saying, "The Lord, He is God! The Lord, He is God!"

The Lord loves to show Himself strong on behalf of those who diligently seek Him, and He is seeking those, today, who will let Him show His power through them. May the Lord impress this message upon each reader of this book, that He alone is the "Wonderful Counselor" and "Prince of Peace" (Isaiah 9:6). As we learn to cast all our emotional burdens upon Him and listen to the Holy Spirit to bring us truth, that truth will set us free and we will enjoy the love, joy, and peace that the world is seeking. God desires each of us not only to be saved, but to be set free to serve Him and to lead the lost into His kingdom.

"Test me now in this," says the LORD of hosts, "if I will not open for you the windows of heaven, and pour out for you a blessing until there is no more need." Malachi 3:10

Discussion Questions

1. When you first heard of this ministry did you immediately embrace it? If you did not immediately accept it, what hindered you from accepting it initially?

2. What has been your experience with regard to sharing this ministry with your pastor or with other believers?

3. Do you know many believers who are taking psychiatric medications in order to cope with life and with their emotions?

4. How would your church look if it began to function more like the New Testament Church and began to minister to the emotional and spiritual needs of its members?

5. How do you think it would impact the world if the Church began to genuinely help those with grief, anger, shame, addiction, depression and other emotional struggles, and the world could see the difference?

Personal Application

Each genuine believer is a member of the universal body of Christ, the Church, and the Church is God's agent for impacting the world. Each of us has a responsibility to be involved in a local church and to participate as a member of that church and to help it spread God's kingdom. Consider what you can do to equip yourself to help others and to spread the truth that Jesus is the answer to our emotional struggles and He alone can give us peace.

As you finish this book or this class please do two things to maintain the impact of it in your life. First, consider what you can do to apply these principles to your own life to demonstrate the power of God. Second, consider how you can begin sharing this with others in your circle of influence. As each believer does this we will come into more conflict with the world around us but we will shine as lights in the world. It is, indeed, a dark world without the light of Jesus and "If, therefore, the light that is in you is darkness, how great is the darkness!" (Matthew 6:23). Do as Jesus told us to do in Matthew 5: 16, "Let your light shine before men in such a way that they may see your good works, and glorify your Father who is in heaven."

Prayer Plan Assessment Guidelines

Purpose: To identify life events, and the underlying emotional issues connected to these events, that may be causing some continuing difficulties for the ministry client, and to develop a prayer plan for them to help resolve their feelings of grief, anger, and shame and in order to improve their functioning.

Areas to Address: Each of the following areas should be explored briefly, and then a prayer plan should be developed for resolving each emotional issue identified. While taking notes make an A, G, or S in the margin to identify each potential Anger, Grief, or Shame issue that surfaces.

Parenting
- Who raised them? (parents, grandparents, stepparents, etc...).
- How did the parents and caretakers get along with each other?

- What were each of the client's caretakers like?
- How did the client get along with each of their biological parents and other caretakers?
- How did the client get along with their siblings and other children raised with them?
- Were there any traumas or significant losses before school age?

Childhood

- Did the client enjoy school?
- How did the client do in grade school academically, socially, and behaviorally?
- How did the client do in middle school academically, socially, and behaviorally?
- How did the client do in high school academically, socially, and behaviorally?
- Was the client ever placed outside the home of their biological parents? If so, why?
- Were there any traumas or losses during the client's school years?
- Did the client ever experiment with drugs or alcohol?
- Was the client ever arrested or in trouble at school?
- Did the client graduate from high school? If not, why?

Adulthood

- Marriages: Identify each marriage, the length of the marriage, a summary of each marriage, the problems in each marriage, and children from each marriage.
- Serious Relationships: Identify each serious romantic relationship from adolescence through adulthood including the length

of the relationship, a summary of each relationship, the problems in each relationship, and children from each relationship.

- Has the client ever been arrested?
- Has the client ever used or abused drugs or alcohol? If so, when did it begin, when did it become regular, and when was the last time they used?
- Has the client ever had counseling, mental health problems, taken psychiatric medications, or been placed in an inpatient facility? If so, when and why?
- Has the client experienced any traumas as an adult?
- Has the client experienced any significant losses in adulthood?

Prayer Plan: Write on a 3X5 card the anger, grief, and shame issues needing to be addressed and use this prayer plan to guide you when you pray with the individual. Check off each prayer need once you have prayed with the individual about the issue and they have been set free from it. Continue this until all issues have been resolved.

BIBLIOGRAPHY

Alvear, Diana. "Call for prayers after Rick Warren's son commits suicide." *NBC News*. April 7, 2013. http://www.today.com (accessed April 7, 2014).

Breggin, Peter. Brain-disabling Treatments in Psychiatry. New York: St. Martin's Griffin, 2007.

Breggin, Peter. *Medication Madness*. New York: St. Martin's Griffin, 2008.

Breggin, Peter. *Toxic Psychiatry: Why Therapy, Empathy and Love Must Replace the Drugs, Electroshock, and biochemical Theories of the "New Psychiatry"*. New York: St. Martin's Griffin, 1994.

Carey, Benedict. "Anger Management May Not Help at All." *NYTimes.com*. November 24, 2004. http.//www.NYTimes.com (accessed April 3, 2014).

Corsini, Raymond. *Current Psychotherapies, 3rd Edition, p. 9*. Itasca, Illinois: F.E. Peacock Publishers, 1984.

Cromie, William J. "Half of us suffer from mental illness, survey finds." *Harvard University Gazette*. June 16, 2005. http://news.harvard.edu (accessed September 1, 2014).

Edelson, Eric. "Ron Artest Sr. among those shocked by brawl." *ESPN Magazine*. November 22, 2004. sports.espn.go.com (accessed 2014 April 7, 2004).

Flacus, Gilliam. "Rick Warren acts on mental health in son's death." *Associated Press*. February 25, 2014. Unknown (accessed April 1, 2014).

Genevro, Janice I., Marshall, Tracy, and Miller, Tess. *Report on Bereavement and Grief Research*. Scientific Advisory Group, Center for the Advancement of Health, 2003.

Graham, William F. *Nearing Home: Life, Faith, and Finishing Well*. Nashville, TN: Thomas Nelson, 2011.

Kendler, Kenneth S., John Myers, and Sidney Zisook. *Americal Journal of Psychiatry* (Guilford Press), 2008: 1454.

Kendler, Kenneth S., John Myers, and Sidney Zisook. "Does Bereavement-Related Major Depression Differ From Major Depression Associated With Other Stressful Life Events?" *American Journal of Psychiatry*, 2008: 1449-1455.

Kendler, Kenneth, and Carol Prescott. *Genes, Environment, and Psychopathology: Understanding the Causes of Psychiatric and Substance Use Disorders*. New York: Guilford Press, 2006.

Lilienfeld, Scott. "Psychological Treatments that Cause Harm." *Psychological Science*, 2007, Vol. 2, No. 1.

Neimeyer, Robert and Currier, Joseph. *Current Directions in Psychological Science*, 2009: 352-365.

Schmidt, Alvin J. *How Christianity Changed the World*. Zondervan, 2004.

Shear, Katherine, Ellen Frank, Patricia R. Houck, and Charles F. Reynolds. "Treatment of Complicated Grief: A Randomized Controlled Trial." *Journal of American Medical Association*, 2005: 2601-2608.

Stroebe, Margaret, Henry Schut, and Wolfgang Stroebe. "Health Outcomes of Bereavement." *Lancet*, 2007: 1969.

Warren, Rick. *Pastor Rick Warren's son, Matthew, commits suicide, church says* (April 7, 2013).

Watson, Paul Joseph. "State of Connecticut refuses to release Adam Lanza's medical records." *Infowars.com*. September 24, 2013. www.infowars.com (accessed March 1, 2014).

Made in the USA
San Bernardino, CA
14 July 2018